TRUE LOVE POEMS:

Ode to all American girls
Ode to Naomi Campbell
Trials of Princess Diana
Ode to Bianca and Others

WHISPERS OF Love

TRUE LOVE POEMS

SMITHSON BUCHI AHIABUIKE

Order this book online at www.trafford.com
or email orders@trafford.com

Most Trafford titles are also available at major online book retailers.

All characters in this anthology of true love poems are fictional except a few celebrities and
my mother. Every single poem is simply the author's power of creative imagination with
true life experiences. Any resemblance to real life situation is simply a coincidence.

Print information available on the last page.

ISBN: 978-1-4907-3119-3 (sc)
ISBN: 978-1-4907-3118-6 (hc)
ISBN: 978-1-4907-3117-9 (e)

Library of Congress Control Number: 2014905143

Trafford rev. 03/04/2015

 www.trafford.com

North America & international
toll-free: 1 888 232 4444 (USA & Canada)
fax: 812 355 4082

For my dear sweet mother who died when I was only two years old,
Ada Ada Jane Udensi Ahiabuike (Nee Onuabueke-Ngbalagu Ebule-Ukwu)
Above all, my mom was once real.

For my wife Chinyere, the true gift of God

For Nma, the legendary Virgin Princess of Eluama
For evoking the genesis of these innocent lines
Which were richly inspired by the virgin scenes
Of the panoramic crescent green Kubwa Hills

CITATION

Dear Nma,
"You once said
You are going
To send a poem
What happened?
I didn't see it
In the last letter . . ."

Then I sat down all night long
And wrote the "Midnight Dreams"
And sent to you
But you never replied
And now I have written again
Time and time again
Again, and again and again

But you have remained silent
I looked for you everywhere
But I could not find you anywhere
You were nowhere at my humble reach
And the gap between us is abysm
Then I took solace between the lines
Of my *"whispers of love"*
So long!

CONTENTS

PAGEANT OF LONGER POEMS

UNSEALED LOVE LETTERS

INTRODUCTION

This anthology of true love poems was inspired by real people and written nearly twenty years ago. They span through my period in high school to my time in medical school and several years after. This is more than fifteen years of human interaction and journals. Friends ask me, "What does your wife think of them?" I say, she is indifferent about the poems because they were written long before we knew each other and decided to get married. And to crown it all, she inspired her own long collection of true love poems named after her **Chinyere-Seeding Love;** that will not be published in our life time except if she decides to share it with the rest of the world. Different situations inspired different poems. I was not very lucky with the dating game as my style was too religiously inclined and idealistically spiced with too much romance and poetry without action, the girls do not necessarily like that, and so I buried myself writing down the feelings they inspired. All of the sources of inspiration had no knowledge of it. And I intend to keep it that way. They had no clue that I write poetry with such intensity any way.

I have decided to publish these poems as a gift to the world so that people can appreciate the power of creativity as a substitute important avenue to channel youthfulness and its attendant mischief. The imaginary legendary princess of Eluama came much later as an anchor and the character on which all the emotions were heaped. My village Eluama, inspired me more than anything I can imagine, and it was not a surprise that Nma became a legendary character in the book. The last love poems in the book in the 'unsealed love letters' were closely woven around her as I found her an inspiring character that many beautiful young girls in my village when I was growing up represent in actuality. And frankly speaking, I am unable to write a fictional love poem without a human character involvement.

My mother it appears was a very formidable soft spot for my emotions. I never had a mother's love. She died when I was only two years of age. I am convinced that my continuous ability to write love poems springs from the fact that I miss my mother from deep down the inner core of my being. Many times the love I have for my mother is transferred to Nma, and that enhanced the intensity more than I could imagine ordinarily. This is why I dedicated the book to the sweet unforgettable memories she evoked. Even as a grown adult, I still miss the fact that I never had a mother, especially on my birthdays. The reason is that she is the only one who knows what it took to carry me to term, the pains and the joy it evoked.

The poem that clearly we can discuss with its character is "Ode to Bianca." She was a renowned beauty queen at school. That was when I was in the medical school in the late 1980s in Enugu Campus of university of Nigeria. Others are "Ode to Naomi Campbell," "Ode to the Fulani Girl," "Ode to the American Swallow," "Trials of Princess Diana," "Ode to All American Girls," "Ode to Elegant Daughters of Eluama," "American Fever," and many others.

"The pageant of longer poems" was at the center of my attempt to write as I am moved. I pour my heart without any inhibitions, and it goes on and on and on. My frustration at the power of how much love can intoxicate the human spirit is completely revealed. There was no holding back. I had the utter release of my emotions to the full extent of the passion aroused in my heart. I have no regrets at all that I was able to chronicle my feelings for so long a time and they survived the numerous journeys around the world.

SBA,
Gadsden AL

PROLOGUE

Dear Nma,

Nna woke up from bed and heard the cock crow at the other end. Then, are also the ceaseless panting drops in his bathtub echoing a peculiar rhythm of an old rustic lullaby. The dawn is chilly and cold, and peeping through the window the weather is misty and the cloud is heavily pregnant. "The dawn may usher in a dull new day. Call it a rainy day," he told himself.

"For some nine months now I have restricted my pen. I have refused to write to you because I am very upset about the last unfriendly treatment I got from you. I had questioned myself severally what wrong I may have done to your virgin teenage heart. And I could not put anything together, except that I have refused to die in silence. I have professed the love in my heart with the simplicity and innocence of a babbling year old and the clarity of the rising sun. Every bit of how I felt about you could be seen pulsating in the lines of my poems. Some of them even threaten to jump out of the pages. More so, even the tears of love could be seen flowing across the pages. The words themselves are wet. Even their substance is as palpable as a hypertensive radial pulse. The message is tender, kind, and even as refreshing as the pulp of fresh mango juice, then the endearment that spiced the tempo could awaken Romeo and Juliet from their slumbered sleep.

And lo and behold! I saw the sum of it all gather to form and power a fountain. The waters falling from this fountain are not the kind I have known and seen at Ezeiyi Fountains in Eluama. The waters are not water. The fountain flows from mountains of rock far above my head. The ripples of the falling fountain sing only love songs.

And on top of the green Kubwa Hills, where my love fountain springs, are angels with their immaculate wings singing love songs. Even Venus, the Roman goddess of love and beauty graced the orchestration. Indeed a legendary poetic celebration of the great virtues of this great queen whose name is love. And the stream of this royal fountain follows its natural course miraculously running into giant topographical English alphabets with only four letters just before it emptied into the sea of my left ventricle.

And I marveled at how tears of love could have performed such a herculean task. And I wondered with my little head about this great and enigmatic queen called Love."

> But then the tears of love
> Keep falling and falling
> And the fountains of love
> Keep flowing and flowing
> And the love lark keeps singing
> And singing endless love songs . . .

6:30 am
September 30, 1994
Karu FHA Estate
Abuja

WHAT I HAVE TO GIVE

I will make you a dear offer
One good offer that you cannot resist
I will give you my heart
The way it has never been
I will smother you with love
In a manner you have never been
The kind of love you can never resist
The kind of love you cannot refuse
Because I will treat you so well
10   Such that you cannot let me go
If only you can give me a chance
For this test, then you are in for it
Though I am not a magic man
It is only love that I have to give.

6:40 pm
March 4, 1994
Karu, Abuja

Thinking Of You

When I remember you, what do I see?
I see the diamonds dazzling the blue sea
When blue is all in a rainbow spree
When I smell you, the fragrance is rose
From your soothing smiles the morning sun arose
Making my spirit glitter and blossom a dose
In the echo of the quiet night I hear
Nothing but your stiletto voice so clear
Piercing my veto virgin thoughts so dear
Lacing my day with a moment of laughter
Wetting my lips like raindrops falling clatter
Putting my broken pieces of many parts together
When my early morning dreams really come true
Roving in style like swan, thinking of you.

11:00 am
February 14, 1992
Eastern Nigeria Medical Center
Uwani, Enugu

SOMEONE TO LOVE ME

Since I was born twenty-four years ago
I have never for once seen love flow
I have always had dreams and fantasies though
Of what it may sound for love to crow
Though I have fallen in love once
But my heart was reduced to an ounce
Since then I have been scared like mice
To offer my heart again for another sacrifice
For one thing, I do know very greatly
10   Is that I could give all I can very truly
To experience a little of my love dreams
Pouring over me like a fountain of rainbow beams
Ushering me into a new pinball world
Where I will no longer live in the cold

6:00 pm
March 5, 1994
Abuja clinics
Garki, Abuja

Smother Me With Love

If you know you could light my heart's embers
Then ask me for the key to its chambers
If you are convinced of what true love really means
Then I am someone in search of true love
For if, true love exists somewhere in Kubwa Hills
Then I am very ready with a heart to love
For even if it means turning all the leaves of grass
To find my heart throb somewhere in the clover
Then leave the path for me to truly pass
10   For if there is anything for a true lover
Then I am one lonesome heart in great need
For I will give my last energies to feel loved
For though the world craves for this seed
My heart is wondering whether am too late to be loved

6:35 am
March 15, 1994
Garki, Abuja

In Search Of True Love

I have had many enduring drills
To understand perhaps the least-lasting skills
With which to climb the rugged mountains of love
I have dared to venture across dangerous terrains
In earnest search to behold the lover's dove
To lead me to the love island full of hills and plains
I have had many sleepless nights brooding about love
Many times flying to the blue sky far above
Searching for love in endless white clouds
10   For I have from time and again dreamt of love
For I have crossed many oceans in their winds
For I have dug mines looking for these diamonds
Where the heart of true love was once buried
But when I got there, I was blind and wearied
I had no strength to explore the love caves
For even if Angels come to my rescue in waves
I could only feel my way to the lost treasures
Hidden away from man in the cave of the ancients
Lost to the rubble of the wisdom of the Saints
20   Which tell us to love our neighbors as ourselves

9:50 pm
February 11, 1994
Karu, Abuja

TEARS OF LOVE

Watering my eyes are glass tears of love
The diamond tears of an endless crushing love
For I am in love with a virgin teenage girl
Who does not seem to love me as much
I write her letters every other week
I send her cards every other month
I also buy her presents whenever I can
She never says thank you. She never smiles
When she sees me she prefers to walk away
10   When I want to talk to her
She would rather frown her face
But when I forgot her in search of my star
She was crying and wetting her pillow all night
And I asked myself, "Why is love the way she is?
Why does she pretend when I needed her?"
And when I was gone she kept looking for me
I don't seem to understand all there is to it
Does love really grow and mature in pretense?

8:30 am
March 11, 1994
Karu, Abuja

MIDNIGHT DREAMS

Let me say it all only to myself
For once I set my eyes on a dame
It was like snow falling on oneself
As my aura battled to an enduring game
I swore to keep my thirst only in her vine
For she is a rare gem from a nicety mine.

12:00 Midnight
February 19, 1993
Rimi, Katsina (NYSC)

IN OUR LITTLE SHIP—THE ARGOSY

"What does he have in mind?"
She seems so sure to ask herself
What can I think about myself?
Seeing her looking so young and strong
What on earth can I not think about?
How could it not be the roses on her lips?
What can I not think about, her dropping eyeballs?
Could it not be her, the shiny black hair falling back?
What can I not think about, her volcanic innocence?
10   Could it not be her, the teeth as white as the clouds?
What can I not think about, her double dimples?
What can I not think about, her unusual unique kind
Could it not be her, my ruby, my heart throb?
How can I not think about just what I want?
Tell me please; tell me my pretty young thing
What can I say?
What can I do?
Where can I go?
If not just to say how much I care
20   If not to write poems with letters of her name
Even on the leaves of grass and bark of trees
To tell the world that I am head over heels
In love with a little virgin teenage girl
Who out of the purity of innocence
Is scared of just the man in me
As a distraction to her purity and long ambition
What can I do, even when I know her mind?
And who else on earth can I think about?
Who else can I dream about when I lay my head asleep?

30   What else do I want on this earth if not her?
        And I am scared of being dumped a second time
        Then what can I do?
        Where can I go?
        For I dream great dreams in tears of joy
        When I will sail with her in our little ship
        Then she would have grown much bigger
        With bigger minds, bigger thoughts and greater ideals
        And she can lend me a hand of help
        When I seem to trip and fall in fear
40   Of being dumped in the open sea
        To the joy of the songs of the angry waves
        And in our little ship she named *The Argosy*
        We will sail and sail to our own island
        As the ripples are thrilled in ecstasy
        There will be nothing more to think about
        Except her, just her, just the two of us
        "And what does he have in mind?"
        She still seems to ask her little self
        Even a little more confused than she ever was

12:30 pm
June 13, 1993
In a 504 taxi
Kano-Kaduna Expressway

STREAM OF LOVE

Love flows like a liquid gold in a stream
Which soothes our hearts in an endless dream
Gripping us like an intoxicating venereal wine
Which bares us nude in our own twine
Love is as gentle as the moving clouds
Which brightens our day without any doubts
Leaving us to hover as freely as the swan
To heights where love consumes like a locust swarm

5:00 pm
July 10, 1993
Kubwa Stream
Abuja

Ripples Of Love

On a day at peace in the bed of a stream
Sitting on a rock to fall into a haunting dream
As the talking waters flow with soothing tunes
To cool our days in scenic sand dunes
Where a heart in search of a missing love
A love to keep and watch like the dove
While the busy ripples flow in its little cascades
Flowing to rapids and falls in distinct grades
As the happy leaves wave gently in smiles
10 To thank the winds for their blessings in styles
As the water flows and falls on rocks
As their slapping faces visit many docks
For there comes a time when our hearts are blue
When our love shares the cabins of our crew
To brighten our day at sea on a boat ride
Sailing far and near the waves of the ocean tide
As our hearts are heightened to elevated minds
Then our spirits are spurred to cruise with the winds
As the day is blessed with the warmth of our kisses
20 While our emotions rise and fall with our wishes
With the days warm and busy like the dragon fly
Like our love learns to soar into the evening sky
Just at the very moment we needed it most
To pay for the moments we all seemed lost.

4:20 pm
July 10, 1993
Kubwa Stream, Abuja

SHE I

Like the mist in the early morning rains
Like the rainbow in the white clouds of mist
I witnessed her glorious descent down the plains
When spotless swans fly across in joy of twist
Taking over me like raindrops of love
Pouring down the hills in sun-splashed splendor
Chilling my bones like the early morning dove
Seeking to possess me with a thrill of pleasure
Steering my ship home to the Island of Love
10   For she is the healing breeze from the east side
Like the rainbow spree in the white clouds above
She is the love Scud emerging from the west tide
Aimed directly at my endless lovesick heart
Overwhelming me with her love Scud missile
Beating down the pregnant cloud to Mother Earth
Offering me more than I bargained for a while

8:30 pm
April 19, 1994
Karu FHA Estate
Abuja

LEARNING TO LOVE

Our hearts and our minds in search
Through an endless need for a stretch
We soon learn the great art of love
Like an innocent little child in a grove
For our souls from time that never ends
Craves for nothing but love as life amends
And smoothens the plaques standing on our ways
For when we live and learn to love always
Then our inner minds acquire a new spirit
10   That endures to reap an endless benefit
Not necessarily from the flesh and blood
But more importantly from a heavenly flood
Which searches our minds and thoughts in want
And bless our souls when the needs are sacrosanct

11:54 am
February 2, 1994
Karu, Abuja

On a Certain Girl at School

Nma, you cannot see yourself to make reviews
So I wish to express my feelings in your avenues
To make my emotion-laden point short and clear
You are to me accommodating, attractive and dear
Your company is treasured like gold
Thus my determination to make a go with bold
You are the ideals of my great imagination

So show me your true colors and position
Remember it is not easy to be turned
10   When one's love is not evenly returned
It becomes very difficult and bitter
More so, when one's emotions are in a tether
Though it is neither my fault nor yours
The response to natural impulse sometimes leaves us crushed

12:30 pm
July 27, 1984
Federal Government College
Enugu

THE AMERICAN FEVER

As a boy I used to hum like the bumblebee
Then I fell in love with a girl quite unlike me
We got along and dreamt great and innocent sweet dreams
Our thoughts and aspirations did ripple like great streams
And we proposed to sail on board just the two of us
We battled, we swatted with great inspirations thus
Within the four walls of the Lion's Den on soft green hills
Where great academic drills sublimated with diverse skills
Where Boys and Girls traversed to mature into Men and Women
With an olive-branch as exalted as the flowing fountain pen
10   Here my girl professed how much she loves me like glue
With my innocent heart I was swept away without a clue
That an alien American bug had arrived a night after
Bitten her, infected her, and they sailed away with laughter
Leaving me empty and lonely without even a Dear John letter

May 15, 1993
Block 84, Flat 3 (Comoros)
OAU Summit Quarters
Asokoro District
Abuja

TELL THE HANDS OF THE CLOCK

Tell the hands of the clock
That my chin is smooth without beard
While my hair is dark though grey preferred
Tell the hands of the clock
That my thoughts and actions are shallow
Without the touch of years soft like pillow
Tell the hands of the clock
That I want to be a man and old
Wise like the tortoise as I was told
10   Tell the hands of the clock
That the grip of youth is too hard on me
While my mind cannot crystallize in its plea
Tell the hands of the clock
That she has decided to leave me
Wicked enough because am young and same
Tell the hands of the clock
That wealth which comes with age
Has robbed me of my love on stage
Tell the hands of the clock
20   That am pregnant with youth
While scared of giving birth to a glut
Tell the hands of the clock
That am eager to grow as tall as a shadow
Preferred though a baby with smiles aglow
Tell the hands of the clock
That am young and strong with vigor
And that it should not come to my celebration with rancor

9:30 am
August 3, 1991
Ajuh's house
Doma Road, Lafia

RIPPLES IN MY BATHTUB

Every morning I step into my bath
Warming and soothing my nerves to a path
With myself playing it really nude
With all my appendages feeling rather good
My memory flashed back to Adam and Eve
Wandering and gathering in Eden without a sleeve
Then they later had Cain, Abel, and Seth
And I asked myself how does the sun set
For a wonder super baby to be born
10   First, where is my Eve yet to adorn
A super baby to smile in my arms
Soothing my nerves like the Jordan balms
My heart melts for a young pretty dame
For now, I am scared of the love game
Having dabbled into it and got some boots
Then going back home to trace greater roots
I saw an Eve, young at heart a charming girl
With great a family gene as the marble tile
Will she accept to marry me? I asked
20   For that is a riddle and my task
Though a young lad with less behind
Born with nothing except my unique kind
Searching for someone to share my thought
Hunting for a heart to read my great worth
And equate them not equal to silver or gold
But something worth more than the eyes can behold
Then I ask my God that if a good wonder woman
Be manna, let me have enough just for one man

7:40 am
January 26, 1993
Rimi, Katsina (NYSC)

TEENAGE LOVE

What does a girl see?
When she first falls in love
She sees her first Romeo
As her only husband
On whom she heaps
This enveloping crush
A crush as teenage
As is selfishly grinding
Gripping the inexperienced
10   Fragile teenage heart
In its ugly jaws
For when she falls in love
Just like everyone else does
She plunges into the pool
Whole heartedly headlong
Falling head over heels
In a maiden attempt to love
For an ideal love
Which is nothing
20   But mere dreams
About Prince Charming
Of the old fairy tales
The spotless princess
Of the Sleeping Beauty
The honey pot
Of the busy beehive
The sweet sugar coating
Of the bitter pills
The haunting love
30   The love that never grows

Into the sweetness
Of the utopian
Happy ever after
The fantasy world
Of grandiose imaginations
She grabs it whole heartedly
Without any reservations—
For the colds of a rainy day
For she swallows the bait
40 Hook, line, and sinker
Like a helpless hungry fish
She gets carried away
Into the contagious falsehood
Of first love, a crushing crush
For when the first shot
Rings out into the air
Her heart pounds
Like a pile driver
Her head aches in chimes
50 Like the grandfather clock
Playing tricks on her innocent heart
Vulnerable to pounding bouts
Of experienced older hearts
Who prey on innocent minds
To continue the exploits
Leaving behind some bits
And some pieces
For the compromising
Winds of time
60 To lend a helping hand
To heal the ugly wounds
Of the exploits of first love
The bane of naïve teenage girls
In search of the lost islands
Lost worlds of ideal love
Where men and women
Boys and girls once lived

8:30 pm
July 15, 1993
Kubwa, Abuja

SHE II

She is the ideal of my endless dreams
Flooding my lovesick heart in beams
She is in love with the man in me
Knowing the sweetest herb for my tea
Knowing the value of love not priced for money
She is a beauty as spotless as a baby
She is a gem priced more than ruby
Reading my tender feelings in the brew
Cooling my youthful nerves like dew
10   She is the centerpiece of my heart
Only she could summon the will for a start
She is the epitome of my crave for love
On whom I dream and float endlessly above

6:30 pm
April 24, 1994
Garki, Abuja

A Little Kindness Shows

Our vain human world daily goes
Just like an endless flowing fountain does
For our lives many times fail to stand
When worries seem to take an upper hand
For then, there is a need for this demand
For us to stretch a hand of goodness
Expressing a little gesture of kindness
For our ephemeral world is merely a stage
Where we daily play our parts to age
10   And endure to leave something behind
For when we learn to be nice and kind
Then, God who created us with love
Will stretch his arm as a dove
To bless our souls from above

11:15 pm
February 1, 1994
Karu, Abuja

ODE TO ALL AMERICAN GIRLS

Take a message across the rivers
Take a message across the seas
Take a message across the oceans
Take a message across the Atlantic
Take a message across the Pacific
Take a message to all the American damsels

Tell them I send my love
Like the gentle coos of mother dove
Tell them how wonderful they are
10   Tell them how beautifully they star
Tell them that many times they appear as angels
Dropping down the blue sky like great models
Yes, unique models chiseled out probably from granite
Whose charm many times the streets of New York ignite

Tell all the African-American chicks
Including the Caucasians and Indians in their likes
That I love them all with some kind of craze
Threatening to set the San Francisco Bay ablaze
That I have dreamt dreams
20   As it always seems
When I could visit them in America
All the way from the continent of Africa
And take them out for an evening date
And then teach them how Africans bait
And then have a feel of them
Tell them that when I watch them
Even without paying any pennies

Even with those their Hollywood nannies
That the tongue in my mouth goes watering
30   And the small of my front goes sweating

Tell them I miss them a great deal
That I love them even in Ebony grill
Tell them that though
I don't love Nma any less
But that I could plead so
Just to kiss their juicy lips nonetheless
And pluck their apple breasts as well
Begging to keep only two in my shell

Tell them that I have dreamt dreams
40   And greatly wondered when my dreams
Could really come true
And make me feel less blue
When I could board the airplane
And step on JFK in a joyful train
Just to behold their likes
And we could go on a hike with their bikes

Tell them to help me out
Tell them to rescue me with their clout
Tell them that when I reached their foreign mission
50   For a passage, for my American love expedition
That their mission denied me passage
That my emotions are tethered into limbo rage
That my emotions are swinging into the cloud
That my exploding love for them is crying aloud
Tell them I send all my love like a dove
Tell them about an African boy in love
Pleading endlessly about the love so strong
Eagerly hoping for a protracted date so long

12:45 am
November 23, 1994
Karu FHA Estate
Abuja

THE PRINCESS OF ELUAMA

The ingredients of beauty is 'Ngwa Nma'
The unknown princess who lives on the hills
In the little town of beauty called Eluama
For here in the market square are beauty drills
Performed with silver bangles and gold trinkets
During the famous ceremony when virgin girls
Whose fathers are kings and princes in amulets
Exhibit their wealth of Naira notes in varying styles
When Ngwa Nma, the beauty queen of Eluama appears
From her cocoon of fattening in the beauty rooms
Where men are forbidden without locking their zippers
When the forests of Nneochia swarm with assorted mushrooms
When *Ogbara-ega* and *Okuru-Opara* adore our plains
When the virgin leaves of grass grow without restraints
When the heavens themselves blaze forth from time again
In the market bowl of Ahunta—the public square—
Where the Nobles of Eluama spray their wealth in train
As a human throng carry the princess like a snare
While young men struggle in earnest to catch a glimpse
As these bare royal "princessly" feet kissing the fine sands
Of this revered ceremonial square where the name of shrimps
Rings a bell to mothers whose daughters take new bands
In fulfillment of Ihe-Iriji for a completeness of womanhood
When Ngwa Nma assumes her princessly crown in elegance
In this coronation when young men hold back their manhood
Till it matures to an exalted aura of excellence
When sons of plebeians go merely to entertain their eyes
As such beauty and elegance are leased at cut throat price
Though it is the flamboyant ceremonial Ahia-egwu of old

30   When young maidens win a special prize for womanhood
              Paid with pride by young men who learn to uphold
              That the unknown price of a virgin princess untold
              Is paid by a disciplined fire of manhood

2:25 pm
September 26, 1993
Kubwa, Abuja

ODE TO ELEGANT DAUGHTERS OF ELUAMA

I

Where in the world is Eluama, the little town on a hill?
Where in this wide world is this home of goodwill?
Where babies are born by the hand of God's will
These babies were made by God on the first birthday
When God woke up fresh for the creation day
Then the babies were made by the hand of God
Not from wood or leaves but from the earth mud
Then they were made to pass through raindrops
Pounding endlessly to the rhythm of their downs and ups
10   Thrilling uncontrollably the joyful green jungle leaves
Then the babes grow into pretty girls on sleeves
Then the girls grow into princesses and beautiful women
Then the princesses became the daughters of men
Then these beautiful daughters were spotted and married
To men in different lands, far and wide as varied

II

These elegant daughters are made of iron and steel
Dropping every other day from the cloud endlessly still
They are tested women and not mere pushovers
They are from a royal breed who never wears pullovers
20   They are pretty, well groomed, and beautiful too
They are well nurtured and carefully tutored too
They are no small girls indeed
They are no big girls indeed
They are women, they are mothers
Who merit their prize in golden platters

Women who are women, women of substance
Those women who do not farm for mere subsistence
Women who do not salute each other
By mere act of stretching one another
30   They do not greet by shaking hands
They use their buttocks as their hands
They slap their robust buttocks three on the right side
And then another three on the other left side
Because many of them are title holders in their ranks
Most are celebrities in their own merits and watered banks

III

They could be really charming in their looks
They are women whom men respect not as mere cooks
They are women who command enviable respect
Not only for other women folk to inspect
40   But women polished by men, women of substance
Women as solid as the eagles' stance
Women as bold as a lion's face in a spigot
Women as eloquent and as accurate as a parrot
From a distance I watch them
From a distance I admire them
And many times I ask my little self
What stuff are these women made of?

IV

And I dream dreams that Nma will join
But where Nma refuses to pick on my loin
50   Then whether I find her in America or Britain
She will sure give me a daughter to train
And whether my daughter is married to an American
Or to the East by any man, an Indian
She is by noble inheritance, an Elegant Daughter
Then she will join this Peahen Club with laughter
And bring back home those glories that haunt me
Since I became a teenager at home
These Elegant Daughters where do they come from?
They are from the hilltops and plain-tops kingdom

60   They are daughters born on the hills
       By the wives of kings and princes' mills
       And they look down to others from the valleys
       Because they are born on top of hills like turkeys
       They thrive where kings and princes live
       They live only where great women thrive.

       8:30 pm
       February 20, 1994
       Garki, Abuja

TRUE LOVE

True love never sees any wrong
True love builds to heights from wrongs
True love sees white as always white
Never as brown or as blue may be
True love accepts the wrongs
For what they are
Builds on forgiven wrongs
To make amends
True love is like
10   Endless flowing stream
That gets along
Through rapids and falls
True love sings like the ripples
Cascading gently from the bedrock
Where gentle and tender feelings flow
True love grows like the mustard seed
That springs from pinlike drops
Which germinates on a fertile soil
And grows into a gigantic tree
20   True love never really dies
True love finds more favor
In the eyes of a married couple
True love endures where faults abound
True love accepts the faults as they come
And lends a mending hand for the future
True love never frowns to despise
Rather it reacts as it should
And learns to accept the faults
True love never grows in a hostile mind

30   For the ingenuity of love is tender at heart
True love works like the winds of time
That wakes the sun from sleep to rise
To comfort the lost and lonesome heart
Which broods from many wrongs not forgiven
True love passes like the gentle breeze
That cools the heat and heaviness of the heart
True love is as innocent as a newborn
That seeks for nothing
But the mother's milk
40   True love never wrongs
True love never cheats
True love is humble
True love is caring
True love is gentle
True love loves
True love never discriminates
True love learns to forgive and forget
True love endures in the storm of the sea
True love never abandons the other
50   True love survives a shipwreck
True love shines like the sun
Yes, like the rays of the early morning bloom
True love blossoms like the rose at noon
True love is beautiful and better felt
True love is a queen in a distant land
Which rule where men are weak
And women do even the job of men
True love radiates warmth and joy
True love is as warmly and as weakly
60   As what it really takes to love
True love shines when the day is dull
And warms when the times are hard
She encourages when the going is rough
She rejoices when the going is good
She is enduring in plenty and in need
True love lends a needy hand
When the going is rough

True love builds and never destroys
True love loves from the heart of love
70   And accepts the faults with—
Which we are endowed
True love is peaceful and friendly in distress
True love blossoms
Even in the desert scorch
True love wets the dry lips from want
True love laughs when it should laugh
And cries when there is need to cry
True love always lights the candle flame
When the heart seems to lose the game
80   True love is as plain as the light of the day
True love is as melodious as a music note to play
As the waterfalls from nature's fountains in display
True love is kind
At heart as it may
And as selfless as the clouds
Which always come together
To form rain that falls to the earth
This flows to the kind hearts

As well as to the wicked
And bring blessings
From above unreserved
True love never keeps a diary of wrongs
True love is possessive and a jealous love
This consumes to an enduring point
True love never fights any battle
True love never wins battles
True love never loses battles
100 Though reciprocal as it may
It reconciles with a truce
True love never draws a battle line
True love is never boastful and puffed-up
True love never cries when it should smile
True love is as loving as the dove
True love never learns to cheat in style

True love is faithful and always fair
True love endures for the greatness of tomorrow
True love realizes that nothing comes as easy
110   As the innocent chimes of grandfather clock
True love remains as precious as gold
True love is as pure as the white clouds
And as innocent as the holy birds
Which always flock in a pair
A pair of a male and female folk
Who cherish their treasure very dearly
True love hums like a great songbird
Which sings to console an injured heart
True love thrives with enduring warmth
120   And never leaves the other in the cold.

3:45 pm
July 15, 1993
Middle of a stream
Kubwa, Abuja

ODE TO BIANCA
A CELEBRATED BEAUTY
QUEEN AT SCHOOL

As a boy sizzled with the quest for knowledge
I found myself in the four walls of a medical college
There, the quest for the unknown was really hot
That my life then rotates in a triangular spot
From Room 321-G to the Ransome—Kuti Refectory
Where I oiled my engine to the book factory
Then, all that mattered was book, exams, and passing
The campus chicks may have disliked me without reasoning
For I never looked back at any of them indeed
10   One day, things were on a lighter mood without speed

And behold, I saw a dame, an elegance of beauty
I looked closer and I saw an epitome of African beauty
Walking gracefully to the campus refectory in style
She has a royal carriage laced with a professional smile
Her gentle strides scared the dust off her royal feet
Her regal steps were uniquely unfamiliar to fit
Into one I could easily recall, so I paused
I looked closer to this queen as she passed
Her skin is as fair as the twinkling star
20   Her presence alone in enough alarm in a bar

I followed very carefully with the corner of my eyes
Her face is indeed as electrifying as lightning
As cold chills run down me in goose pimples thrilling

Then her long hair drops down her back in sparkles
As black and as romantic as a girl in love twinkles
For reasons unknown to me I was really scared
Seeing this human species of exceptional breed
For indeed what I saw I must tell the world
For when I got to ROOM 321-G I recalled

30 "Oh Man" you can't believe me today
What I saw my eyes never did yesterday
She is as tall as the high clouds
She is as elegant as the Beauty in the crowds
Her skin is as fair and unlike a Nigerian
Her hair is as long and as dark as an Indian's
She is as pretty as anything I never saw
Her eyes are as sensual as a seashore
She walks with only regal steps in rhyme
And her speech is like those in Newcastle upon Tyne
40 They say she is the Nigerian Beauty Queen
Who has won many accolades since she was eighteen
She must have been a royal breed
Who was born and nurtured for this need
For her skin is as spotless as the day olds
On her lips lilies grow and wrap into folds
Her legs are as romantic as those in Hollywood
As I stared still admiring her like a stump of wood
I even forgot that I have a lecture to attend
For when I recalled my whereabouts, I decide to pretend

50 That indeed all is well with me, for this rare opportunity
To behold this renowned world acclaimed Queen of Beauty
For they say her name is Bianca which means Beauty
For they say she is a gem as previous as a ruby
For they say her father is the lord of the manor
For she was born with a silver spoon in her incisor
For they say her sweet heart is a celebrated man of valor
As I pulled my little self out of this romance
I was scared of having seen a goddess in a trance
For such beauties never grow in all lands

60   Except beside the ocean waves on sea sands

9:30 am
September 24, 1989
Room 321G
Mazi Mbonu Ojike Hall
University of Nigeria
Enugu Campus

IN SEARCH OF A FULANI GIRL

Tall, graceful, long hair, a brown skin
Good manners, good education, solid profile
The daughter of a member of the house
Yes! A Fulani girl haunts his youthful imaginations
Where is she? The product of an African gene
Where could she be found, the African beauty
Who has seen her the minister's daughter
His youthfulness searches for this unknown queen
He takes off to the streets of Jos
10 Everyone he sees, he begins to ask
No one seems to know where she is
He moved round the town on foot and in a taxi
Until he became possessed by an unseen, and
And an unknown spirit of a Fulani girl

It was on a youth day, he zooms off
To the stadium in earnest search for her
But to no avail, and his friends laugh at him
And say, "When you see her, 'Fulani girl'
Will be written on her face," but he did not give up
20 He wandered in the university campus to no avail
He picks up his history books to read about these rare genes
By the time he finished he became more possessed
So he kept searching, though a trip to the grass plains
May give a clue to the homes
Of this wandering race, but he insists on the groomed
A trip to the Fulani market in Fofure near Yola
Revealed assorted species of these African queens
The young man stood at the corner, observing them,

Taking pictures and studying this enchanting race
30   By the end of it all it was obvious to him
That this wonderful queen of the savannah
Could not communicate in a universal language
They were not groomed, but all the other qualities
Were there except a few
He was hot inside him and mad with the rulers
He thought of a way to steal her and tame her
And then keep her, but it was impossible
So he went home to the east with a heavy heart
At a point he let off the steam in emotions and wondered!
40   What a wonderful race with great genes still lost
In the rubble of their past—nomadic wandering life
But suddenly he wakes up from this romantic trance

7:30 am
August 27, 1990
2 Barrow Avenue
Ikoyi, Lagos

TREASURE HUNT

I left home to the deserts
In search of peace in oasis hearts
To bare by dreams and battered haunt
And drill my psyche for a diamond hunt
And as wretched as a man wearisome
I found myself young and handsome
I dug the desert sand dunes
I listened to the desert heat tunes
My gold mine is far underneath
10   From the reach of my panting breath
Then a lost lone girl pilot
Ran out of luck in the desert pot
Crash landing in my blue oasis
I nursed her to smiles from crisis

She was young and pretty like a spring
She gave me a compass diamond ring
And opened my clouded eyes
After years of being locked in ice
What I sought in the desert dust
20   In the bowels of the earth crust
Dropped down beyond the clouds
I was let loose from my cold bounds
To fly like the free Thorn Birds
Who were once lost from their wilds
With their withered feathers for generations
All of a sudden their will and devotions

Changed them into beautiful white swans
Free and fruitful like the desert wind vans.

7:30 am
December 13, 1992
Rimi, Katsina (NYSC)

ODE TO A FULANI GIRL

Since he was a little boy in high school
His psyche has been haunted by the stool
The royal throne made of silver and gold
On which the queen of Africa sits untold
Unknown to the world of our great times
Uncelebrated in the cold of luster chimes
Singing endlessly about her uniqueness on the plains
Where beauty and elegance on bridal trains
Storm the world in a trance of beauty queens
Haunting his mind as a boy since his teens
Only to appear before him in his consulting room
After years and endless months of searching for the broom
Recounting her many parts in endless love dreams
When the moon lighting glows with her ineffectual beams
For she is as elegant as a lady
For she is as precious as a priceless ruby
As graceful and as sensual as a princess
And as great and as influential as power prowess
She is as slim as a pole
She is as tall as a tree
Her skin is as fair unlike a mole
Her hair is as dark and as free
As her face is as fair and as pretty
And as charming as nothing but beauty
She is an epitome of an African woman
She is as polished and as good as a Roman
She is the end of his dream world
Consulting him unannounced with bold
The sight of her spurs his pulse racing fast

30   In his endless search in the past
For this great African queen of enchanting folklore
Like this polished Fulani girl not seen before
And he told himself, "Whatever barriers stand
On my way to win her heart cannot withstand
The power in the force behind my love
For they will be blown away like a grove"
For she is as sweet as honey
For she is as young as a pony
With the dew drops falling from her eyes
40   Melting the snow in her block of ice
She must be the queen of the savannah
She must have fallen from heaven like manna
She must have been the cream of his dream
Visiting his banks like an endless stream
For she is so pretty
For she is an elegance of beauty
She looks so wonderful and great
She looks as good as a treat
For she has stolen his heart
50   Leaving his head bare without a hat
With the magnetic aura she radiates
Even pulling him along with her mates
In search of his million-dollar queen
Living not too far off in the evergreen
In the gripping aura of love
Hovering around him endlessly like a dove
Seeking to possess his empty heart as immaculate
And as white as the clouds can emulate

10:30 pm
Consulting Room 1
Abuja Clinics Ltd
Garki Abuja

WHEN GIRLS FALL IN LOVE

In one country in Africa
A girl never falls in love
If the guy cooks with kerosene stove
The greater the potentials of wealth
The greater the aura of love is felt
In the ugly attempts to perform
The searching minds of men deform
For the men are driven off
Their natural course
10   In attempts to stuff
What it really takes of course
To win the love of their hearts
For when they are yet pushing carts
The girls never really fall in love with them
But when they push a lotus cart at whim
They cluster around them like sugar ants
She will rather die than not get what she wants
For when the going is rough for a man
He never remembers the love in a woman
20   For when the going gets flashy even an inch
They even itch to be allowed to put your stitch
Just to give her a chance to taste the sugar
Like the ants who abhor the taste of vinegar
Some even argue with the priest in the alter
For they believe in "For Better"
And have no share "For Worse" to come later
For young men are even scared
To bare their minds when snared
By the taste of our girls who even say

30   "Who would want to suffer in May?"
When the sun is hot overhead
When others are enjoying instead
Going to church in flashy Mercedes-Benz cars
While they endured to trek with scars
To bare their foot in agony of a pledge
Making it hard on a rough hammer sledge
Who does not like good things?
After all we are all human beings
Born with the will to admire and appreciate
40   Good and tasty things as we cultivate
The urge to love and be loved like the Americans

3:30 pm
July 15, 1993
Gwagwalada Crescent
Phase II Site I
Kubwa, Abuja

THE BITTER TRUTH

Listen
My sweet heart
For many ceaseless and fruitless brooding
For many countless and lonesome moments
For many endless and crawling days
For many hopeful and passing weeks
For many boring calendar months
For all the poetic celebration chasing shadows
I have lived and dined on illusions
10   I am falling victim of my own haunting ideals
I have been severally haunted by my own creations
I am falling in love with my own imaginations
Though walking down the rubble of memory lane
Spiced with all its countless ups and downs
The rain has poured and heavily too
The dust has settled to Mother Earth
Revealing the bitter and glaring truth
It has eventually dawned on my helpless self
That you are my true and true love
20   That you are my real hopeful love
The one I can lean on even on a rainy day
The kind of love every man craves to have
The kind of love every woman dreams about
The kind of love everyone can greatly count on
An enduring kind of love
But I am trapped and deeply in love
With a teenage beauty I met some time ago
When our love went sour
For she has a strong grip

30   Deep down my heart
Sad enough she bluffs me with disrespect
But I have kept trying over and over
Because I cannot let go the steam
If you can please forgive me
For I do accept
That I do not fully understand
All there is in love
For my heart is in love with someone else
My heart is after another girl
40   And her name is Nma
This is the bitter truth.

9:15 pm
September 19, 1994,
Karu FHA Estate,
Abuja

EAST OF KUBWA HILLS

Looking close into her charming eyes
From a mirror in her youthful face
He saw it all east of green Kubwa Hills
A land swarming only with virgin girls
Who gather every morning at the peak
Of the Kubwa green hills
For a ceremonial bath with the queen
The empress ruling east of Kubwa Hills
For here men are not needed
10   Not even angels are ever required
For a woman to be conceived
And bring forth another virgin girl
For the queen of the east of Kubwa Hills
Was made from a special genetic clone
For she does no other work
Then to bring forth into the world
Princesses whose beauty sends the clouds
To their knees as they bow each morning
To kiss the hills in admiration
For this unique crop of virgins
20   Do not even know that men exist
Not even far to the west of green Kubwa Hills
For in the west boys and girls are born
And they grow into men and women
As in the real world of our twenty-first century
And in the west of Kubwa Hills
Virgins are never born
For they are even seduced in-utero
In their mothers' wombs as babies

In envy by the gods of the east
30 Who are starved by their lust
For the fruitless fruits of the flesh
Which has long been deleted
And reduced to obsolete acts
In the superhuman minds
Of the beautiful virgin princesses
Who live east of the Kubwa Hills
Where beautiful virgin maidens
Grow endlessly on mountain tree tops
And there are no men to spoil them
40 With the obsolete act of lust and passion
And they are left only
With the tongues of the clouds
Who kiss their nipples in rituals
Every cold morning before sunrise
While they weep in ecstasy
With the dripping tongues in sympathy
Going crazy with the morning dew
In their world where men are unknown
To explore the treasures
50 Harbored in their virgin jungles
Leaving love poems here and there
On the chosen leaves of grass
Telling the princesses how beautiful they are
And stirring them into an obsolete
World of men, women, and passion
West of the green Kubwa Hills

8:30 pm
September 27, 1993
Kubwa
Abuja

LOVE IN KUBWA HILLS

Nma!
Could you hear the voice of a love lark?
Singing endlessly like a robin in the dark
Echoing like the swan in a love park
Shining like the star in love plains
Where larks sing their songs without gains
Whispering the tale of love into our ears
Learning to love again without fears
Time after the fire was forced into the winds
10   In earnest attempts to call back our minds
Chorusing the song of love again
After the lonesome interlude of rain
For we seem to lose and to regain
Nma!

Sing me a love song like the larks do
If only you could read my mind in dew
For now and again I do meditate
How much effort one puts in state
To convince a girl how much he cares
20   As many times he learns to make repairs
Of the bits and pieces in his broken hearts
As you may as well make it fly like bats
Into the charming blossom of your looks
Where men have learnt to fish without hooks
As we continue our endless search in the wind
In our world where they say "love is blind"
For men have learnt to love not with their eyes
Rather with their hearts, not anymore with tears

For I am in love with the crescent green Kubwa Hills
30   Harbored irresistibly in your dreaming eyeballs

6:00 pm
September 24, 1993
Kubwa,
Abuja

SHE III

Of all her mother's diamond tears of love
Her dove's heart spurs her on like above
Of all the excitement back at home
Her lion's heart tells her to come
Of all boulevards she admires the crescent
Of all exposures she appears so innocent
So adventurous yet so young
So beautiful yet so strong
Left so much to see so small
10   Let so much lie to answer a call
Fame for one young a pretty mellow
Fit enough to answer a "Junior American Hero"
Though all the differences we greatly share
I do sincerely send all my love with care

10:30 pm
November 29, 1994
Garki Abuja

For Susan Miller (American Peace Corps)

RECIPE FOR LOVE

If you are still searching
For a sweetheart to love
Never give all you have
If each time you give one half
Then you must keep one half
If sometimes you let go
Never allow the bait to drop
Still hold on to it
For while you play
10   Never all your arrows at a time
For if there will be no more thrill
There will be nothing left
Nothing for the rainy day
No more little surprises
No more closed door of suspense
No more empty rooms to search
In that wonder world of love
For when all your arrows
Have fled from your quiver
20   Then the love is supersaturated
There will be no more to guess
No more fantasies to hold on
No more dreams to dream
For a budding love is a game of suspense
For when you are in search
Of a heart to call your own
Never give all you have
Or you will lose out again
Like the true love beads

30   Falling cats and dogs
Like the pelting snow drops
Of my petals of rose
Let go, but hold on!
This is my medicine for love.

5:00 pm
February 15, 1995
Corporate Restaurant
Area 11, Garki
Abuja

TRIALS OF A SPINSTER

How does your heart beat?
Why do you keep awake?
What makes you so restless?
Why are you so lost?
Tell me, my dear spinster
Why are you so carried away?
In the thoughts and dreams
Of the elusive Mr. Right
Why bother so much
10   Remember that every single day
Has her own sunshine
Every ocean has her own waves
Every fountain has her own ripples
Every eye has her own lashes
Every heart has her own desires
Every man has his own wife
Every woman has her own husband
Your day will surely come
When it will come
20   Then you will walk through
The church aisle holding Mr. Right
For your own man
Yes, that man meant for you
Is just somewhere in the corner
No one can take him from you
Never keep sleepless nights
Never even bother looking for him
For when the time comes
He will drop down from the clouds

30 Just like the rain without much ado
 For God sees and hears our cries
 For when the time is ripe
 He gives to every woman
 Her own desired man
 Never you despair, my dear
 For your time will surely come
 Even sooner than you expect

 8:45 pm
 February 19, 1995
 Garki, Abuja

 For Lizzy Ajadi
 For her lust for poetry

"MAKE A BETTER PLACE"

In my mind's eye
I see them all
Children who will heal the world
Innocent little boys and little girls
With the heart of a white dove
Gathering from all corners of the globe
They are living together
They are learning together
They are laughing together
10   They are playing together
They are singing together
They are walking together
They are sharing and eating together
I see them all
They are brown
They are red
They are white
They are chocolate cream
They are ebony
20   They are colored
They are of all the human race
They are Africans
They are Americans
They are Chinese
They are Japanese
They are Asians
They are Indians
They are Europeans
They are Australians

30   They are Eskimos
       They are from all corners of the earth
       They are from all nations of the world
       They know no more color difference
       They are all one human family
       They have lost their racial perception
       They are now racially color blind
       They all have candle lights in their hands
       They also have joy and laughter
       They also have peace and happiness
40   Their candle flames lit the world
       For all arms are no more
       For all wars have ceased to be
       For all human faces lit the world
       With thunderous joy and laughter
       That remains all forever after
       Then these angelic children
       Healed the broken world
       Then they made the world
       A better place
50   For you and for me.

       8:15 am
       February 26, 1995
       Karu, Abuja
       For Michael Jackson
       With Love

Ode To Intimidations
Of Feminism

There comes a moment in a man's lifetime
The routes of his strife sublime
Yielding to the desires of his inner heart
Swallowing feminist intimidations as bluffs of want
A girl is in love with a man
She puts up a face of suntan
While her heart melts on a pan

Now, in the women liberation era
Feminism asserts herself like a penumbra
10   And demands to be treated in equal platform
As the average chauvinist male deform
Though her heart is after yours
She hides in some ugly jaws
Playing hard to get "that flaws"

For when a man loves, his heart glows
Girls lock their feelings in empty bowls
Pounding their face in nauseating indifference
Pretending that indeed all is down in pretense
Feminism is a weak heart
20   That shadows her love hearth
Masking her desires under wealth

For a man, even with his inherent chauvinism
His heart in love glows like a glass prism
He pours out his heart in poetic rhymes
In search for love he really mimes
For men love from depths
And their glove fills the crypts
Leaving no vacuum in the scripts

Feminism in women liberation aura
30   Builds a platform with a pinhole camera
From where she many times hastens in anticipations
Should the man's spirit suffer feminist intimidations
She sends her friends on errands
To reactivate the dampened demands
Refracting some ineffectual rainbow bands

Hoping the reflection of their desires
Will glow as the man requires
Sending a welcome signal of suppressed love
At a time the fellow drops his glove
40
Making fresh battles in aimless delays
When a man's heart burns out in replays

No need for the intimidations of feminism
For this is a man's world without catechism
As a man baring his heart in black and white
Desires to be followed outright
For the feminist defense
Leaves some ugly scars of defiance
Puncturing a man's ego confidence

If Nigerian girls could love without hanky-panky
50   They will sure have a better deal less snaky
Blossoming in sincere contacts, enkindling embers
Not letting men go with weary and empty chambers
Stretching a hand of welcome

Whenever there is need to overcome
Allowing the love of our hearts to become
Making reservations for a rainy day to come

2:10 am
May 7, 1995
Wuse, Abuja

ODE TO WEDLOCK

A time does come
When men feel broody
When some things like rum
In lustful protest make us moody

And overwhelm our spirit
When we feel like loving
Dreaming of a baby to fit
When we sense something

Make endless wars inside
10   Asking questions without answers
Calling us daddy at the mirror side
Making us break saucers

In the haunting suspense of mind
For then a young woman
May utter a reproach of a kind
Roughening the bearded man

Then the inner fire of procreation
Daily haunts for an acquaintance
A woman fit for recreation
20   A lady fit for public acceptance

A choice walking the aisle
In watered eyes of matrimony
There comes a step in a mile
When a man is lonely without money

When his psyche is empty and lonely
When all there is *is alone*
When the hunger to love comes truly
And he daily asks God's throne

In sincere supplication
30   Begging the Almighty God for a wife
To fill the emptiness of isolation
And sanctify a matrimonial life

When men assume responsibility
When men can live a clean life
When men's prayers have specificity
When men's heart beat without strife

And youthful exuberance is a past
For then we are new
Blessed and sanctified in steadfast
40   For all excesses of youth are due

And the emptiness of the past is gone
For we look forward with hope
When the promised future is born
Counting all our blessings down the slope

8:20 pm
May 7, 1995
Wuse, Abuja

PAGEANT OF LONGER POEMS

———◦❖◦———

LOVING SOMEBODY WHEN SOMEBODY CAN'T LOVE YOU BACK

BUT THEN SHE LEFT HIM

Back then when they were kids
Little boys and little girls
They had just left high school
Then she was so young and tender
She was as innocent as a dove
Then she had a clean heart
She could not look into his eyes
She was shy, he didn't know
That she was in love
10   Way back then he didn't know
She was innocently in love with him
Way back then her heart was clean
As clean and as pure as a lamb
The innocent lamb without blemish
Then they met, and then they became friends
Then they were going together
They were so much in love
For he never knew what is love
For he was rather in love with the books
20   For then did he really fall in love
Later, he went into the university
Somehow they lost touch of each other
And they were temporarily separated
By the twin brothers of distance and time
But then the innocent winds of love
Brought them together again
This time around within the four walls
Of a great university on soft green hills
Where they rediscovered themselves

30   Where he also fell in love
For then did he know
Or could he say more correctly
He felt the winds of love
Pass through his inner minds
For she was his first true love
Then her lips were as soft as silk
The pulp of her fingers were as tender
As loving, as caressing, as sensual
As anything as good as love
40   For he saw in her eyes
That she was deeply in love
That she was in love with him
He read from her kiss
From her sweating palms
That she saw her dream man in him
Young and inexperienced as he was
He never saw the handwriting on the wall
He fell in love like he never did before
Like a teenager he was at heart
50   So he plunged into the pool of love
Without any reservations for the rainy day
She was everything perfect to him
Other charming campus chicks
Never stirred his innocent feelings
To change his mind and steal a bit
For then he does not even know
What it means to cheat in love
For he was a perfectionist
Though he was a busy medical student
60   He still made time to see his love
He wrote verses on her lips
He wrote sonnets on her face
He wrote poems on her hair
He did tell her many sweet nothings
For on her face is beauty
For on her lips red roses grow
For on her bed princesses lie

Her laughter rings like a bell
They had a wonderful time together
70   He remembered taking her in his arms
While she screamed to alight
At other times they held the trunk of trees
And chased each other round and round
Sometimes they did hide-and-seek
Running and laughing on top of their voices
While their youthful lungs ached
Many a time they went out to restaurants
Where they ate what his pocket money could buy
And he told her great stories as they dined
80   Those great stories grandmother told him
Sometimes he wrote love poems for her
For she was the only princess that he knew
She was the honey in his bread
She was then his pot of gold
She was his early morning sun
He saw her in the glory of the setting sun
He remembered whispering into her ears
Many a time "Baby, I love you'
Then once she did tell him
90   Something he never really heard
But when he brought his ears closer
She whispered, "I love you too"
To dampen his excitement
She did bite his earlobe
He did cry out with a yell of joy
That was under a mango tree
Beside the female hostel
Many more times, many a time
He did whisper many sweet nothings
100   Into her unadulterated ears
Then she could only smile shyly at him
With those peculiar dimples
On those innocent rosy cheeks
And not for once did he hear her
Call out his name

Whenever they are together
He never really knew why
He has had to wonder
Why she never calls his name
110 For now the memories of the love
The innocent love they shared
Sometimes brings tears down his eyes
For then he was in love like a dove
For then he did build many castles
In the thin nothingness of air
Which sustains our breath of life
Then he did write volumes of letters
Pouring his poetic heart into his lines
Lavishing his love and innocence
120 Savoring the exploits of youth
Just between the lines
Where he pleaded to the goddess of love
To protect his girl from the evils
From the evils those men do
To the hearts of young girls
For he was afraid of losing her
For he made his plans
As he has always done
And also left a space
130 For the comforts of his queen
His mistress in the making
For he called her his mistress
Yes, the mistress of his dream home
Yes his dream home, "The Lilies"
His dream creative home
His dream home
His home where lilies grow
Where lilies grow on the walls
Where lilies grow in the kitchen
140 Where lilies grow in his bedroom
Where lilies grow in his study
Where lilies grow on his dining table
Where lilies grow and change forms

Where lilies change their colors
From green to blue and pink
Where lilies even change their names
Where lilies alter their shapes
And sing songs only in rhymes
Which keep him very busy
150   With his golden pen
Pouring down inspirations from everywhere
In his Lily Cottage where verses grow
Where his thoughts and inspirations
Will haunt the minds of men
Men, women, boys, and girls
Who may take time off to read
The ideals of his home—The Lilies
For he did tell her his dreams
How they could improve their lots
160   Making a home for themselves
Then tears of joy formed in her eyes
From her innocent eyes
Then he saw his little self a superstar
The only guy who could rule her life
And indeed get what he wants
Not only what he wants
But also what is best for him
His head swells like a coconut
Then he plotted his graphs
170   As he always does
And he said to her
"My dear princess
Let's get married today
And make our home tomorrow
Two boys for you
Two girls for me"
For they talked and agreed
That after graduation from school
He will take a trip to a new land
When the dust has cleared
180   He will let her know

When to come to him
For then it will be
Just the two of them
For they could make it
Just the two of them
She held him close to herself
As he unveiled his dreams
His great dreams about tomorrow
Tears of joy from her innocent glands
190   Did wet his shoulder in her emotions
For she dreamt dreams with him
For they dreamt dreams together
And they nodded in affirmation
To their grandiose dreams
Though they were only students
They had great plans for the future
For their hearts were innocent and pure
Though they loved each other greatly
Something bad happened to them
200   For just from the blues
Just from the cold blues
A bombshell was thrown
A bomb he never saw
A bomb he never heard about
A bomb he never envisaged
A bomb he never dreamt about
Was aimed straight to his innocent heart
Then he saw his heart bleeding
His princess has cheated him
210   She has drank from the forbidden river
Which God said they must never drink
Unless and until they were declared
Man and wife before a priest
But she drank the water prematurely
Then she became drunk
Her innocent face disappeared
Her dove's heart was soiled
Then she may have seen a few evils

The evils he never allowed to come his way
220 The evils he has never seen or known
They say it is a fever
They say it is a feverish wave
They called it the American fever
So she caught the American fever
The fever caused by a virus
A virus borne by the dollars from America
Then she never wanted to see him
When he went to see her on Valentine's Day
He saw another boy in her arms
230 Savoring the flavor of a new love
It was the worst experience
That has come his way
In the very recent times
Though she accepted his valentine gift
Things were never the same again
She told him right into his face
That she has now found a new love
That they cannot make it together
That he is as young as a lamb
240 And as penniless as a church rat
That he is a penniless guy
That his head is full of nothing
But the exploits of conquered books
That she cannot marry him anymore
"Not anymore, not anymore"
She took her time to emphasize
She did lie to him
That her mother swore to hang
If she married a poor guy like him
250 A poor young man, as young
As ambitious, as book conscious
As poor, as his poor penniless self
Then he went with his youthful heart
He pleaded for leniency in her courts
He swore to work hard all his life
With every nerve in his brain

With every fiber in his muscles
To earn more than enough
To make their dreams come true
260 His dreams, his mistress, his ideals
Then he pleaded with the goddess of love
To spare him this single shame
He blamed her for bringing him out
Here in the open, in the cold
In a lonesome road, in the public
In the minds of his contemporaries
And then abandoned him in meanness
Then he asked again and again why? Why?
He could not get any answers
270 He searched in the rising sun
He searched in the setting sun
He searched for her in the rocks
On the seaside, in the Nsukka Hills
On the soft green hills
Of their university campus
She was nowhere to be found
He could not anymore find his princess
He could not anymore see his heart throb
She was gone, though not with the winds
280 She was gone, maybe on a train journey
He tried to console his poor self
She must have gone to a new land
Where he could never lay his hands on her
Where he could never kiss her lips again
Where he could no more hold her hands
She was mean, meaner than Jez
Then his princess became a heart breaker
More sinister than Lady Macbeth
Then his princess told him boldly
290 Into his face
That she cannot anymore
Not anymore,
Not any longer
Love him again

That she found a new love
Very bluntly, very meanly
Very, very mean, as mean
As mean and as wicked
As the devil he has never seen
300   Not even heard people talk about
He pleaded with her for pardon
But she hardened her heart
When he asked her his crime
She said he did not reply her letter on time
And that he did not do anything wrong
That she is tired of him
That she intends to explore the world
Just on her own
That she does not need his help anymore
310   Just like that, just like that
In a broad daylight
No comforting words
No pity, no pains in her heart
No guilt, no conscience
Right here beside a church
Then it dawned on him
That they were actually standing
Right beside the church
Then he knew it was
320   The hand of God
He knew she was not his Juliet
She was not his princess after all
She was not his destined mistress
Though he still loved her greatly
Then he pleaded to God
To reverse this ugly trend
But she told him it was impossible
Then he pulled his nerves together
Kept back all the tears
330   Behind the rivers in his brain
And bid her farewell
It was a bitter and a painful farewell

For the unreserved love he had for her
He gave her his last blessings
Though right inside his little self
He know he still loved her dearly
But then she left him.

10:00 pm
February 14, 1990
University of Nigeria
Nsukka Campus

When The Love Died

The love died not when
She refused to see him
The love died not when
She cheated in the dark
The love died not when
He caught her in another man's bed
The love died not when
She slept on another man's arm
The love died not the day
10   He nearly lost his head
The love died not when
He resolved never to see her again
The love died not even
During her wedding day
The love died not with the tears
Coming down his youthful eyes
The love died not even months
After she got married to another man
The love died not when
20   He could not reach her lips
The love died not when she said
"We could not be friends"
Not when she said "It is all over"
The love lived on and on and on
The love could never die
He consoled himself
The love he knows still burns

In his memories of old
The love still haunts him
30 When he remembered their days
Their days clouded with the purity
And innocence of romance
Their days not soiled by the lust
Of the exploits of youth
Their days which were as white
And as clean as MacLean
Their days which could wake
The dead from their graves
For the love of her gracefulness
40 Her great womanhood
Sweeps out memories
From the inner chambers
Of any man's softer parts
For on that faceless day
Coming back from the airport
To pick up his uncle
On the day the cloud was misty
On the day that there was rain
On the day he woke up
50 From his bed
With memories and verses
Ringing in his head
Was the day he was told
That she now has a child
That was the day it dawned on him
That his love is gone
This time around with the winds
That he cannot anymore love
For just what it takes
60 For she has endured
To carry another man's seed
In that sacred womb
Which could have carried his genes

In its purity and innocence
On that day right in the car
From the airport
Was this sad news
Broken to his lovesick heart
On that day he accepted
70   That he is no more in love
On this day did he wonder
And ask himself
"What is this griping aura called love?
Who is this great enigmatic queen?
Whose name is Love?
What is the medicine for love?"
On this day did his love
For her die
His first love died
80   On this day he named Love
For love is like the leaves of grass
A time comes
When they grow to green
A time comes
When they wither to brown
Today his love withered
To the color of brown
This day something great
Frankly did happy to him
90   For a rope, an ugly rope
Was let off his innocent neck
From the pursuit
Of the painful shadows of love
For the true life love
He once cherished greatly died
For now he is scared
He may never really love again
For his true love was carried away
Into other distant lands

100   By the benevolent wings
       Of the winds of time
       Where he could never ever
       Not anymore ask for more

       10:00 pm
       July 8, 1993
       Abuja Airport
       Gwagwalada Abuja

THE LOVE WE SHARED

My heart years for Rimi
My memories long for her
For the love we shared
For the memories of sharing
For the memories of healing
For the memories we evoked
For the memories of poems
The memories that run on hills
For the memories of our night walk
10   Along the narrow tarred roads
Where we stopped sometimes
Beside the Suya barbecue joint
Speaking some spattering Hausa
We have picked in the weeks
My memories are fresh and alive
Like the pulp of fresh mango juice
My memories run down the rocks
The Jibiya dams, the lakes, the banks
The night trips to Niger Republic
20   The desert countryside where we were
Where we selflessly served our country
With a spirit of oneness
For here her name is Rimi
Here did we cook our food
Here did we share our meals
Here did we quarrel along
Here did we settle our differences
Not long before the sunsets
Here I worked and worked

30   Like I never did work
    Like I never did before
    Here did I heal the sick children
    Here did I learn that children
    Are great gifts from God
    Here did I greatly love them
    Here I wished I could afford
    To have my own baby
    For I envied young couples
    Who attend my pediatric clinics
40   With their little daughters in their arms
    With their little sons on their backs
    With their emotions swinging high
    For the life of their little child
    "Doctor, will he be all right?"
    They asked with mist in their eyes
    Here did she come on weekends
    To spend some time with me
    Here did she cook our meals
    Here did she learn to stay alone
50   While I kept awake writing all night
    Here did she push me around
    Just like a woman should
    Here did I learn to love
    In times of peace and war
    Here did I work like a horse
    Just for my only dear country
    The Mbadiwe kind of work
    For here you work without pay
    Though I could barely afford
60   What we did eat
    That was all I could do
    Fear was thrown into me
    For I asked myself
    Could I not afford
    What it takes to care for a woman?
    What it takes to make her happy
    Though I wanted a baby

To smile in my arms at will
Rimi has a nostalgia in me
70 Like the haunting memories of childhood
For the early morning sandstorm
Rocking endlessly on my door
For the bone-chilling desert cold
For the abundant fresh tomatoes
To cook and make fast stew at will
With which we ate our yam
My favorite African food
For here the day is bright
As bright as the morning sun
80 For I am fully on my own
For I am fully in control
For here I explored the world
In its full in want and need
For here I learnt the tricks of love
For here I fell in love at will
She took some time to study me
The man in me, the conglomerate
The complex composition in me
My moods, my anger, my shouts
90 My real self as she could see
My love, my dedication, my cares
For she loved me like I did
For we shared our love
Like the doves
We shopped to fill our fridge
We planned to get along
But at the end of eleven months
They said it is time for us to part
'How could we part?' I queried
100 After all this love we shared
Why should we not stay
Why should we not spend
All our years with each other
Plan our future, have our kids
Why do I want to go back to school?

To continue my empty life
For now I am a man
For I am no more a child
Though I want to excel
110   Though I want to be known
They say I have to leave Rimi
I had no option than to leave
For I parked my bits and pieces
And headed home for good
Where is home after all?
For I queried my little head
Could it not be where joy is?
Could it not be where happiness is?
Could it not be where a man is happy?
120   For I schooled my little self
That home is really everywhere
For in Rimi I did find a home
Though it could not last to time
And I had to go somewhere
But the memories linger hard
The memories I could not shed
For many a time I do remember
For many a time I do long
For many a time I do recall
130   For many a time I do sob
With tears of love rolling down my cheeks
For I felt it really down my cheeks
For I felt it really strong in me
That an important part of me
Was left behind in Rimi
For the memories of the love we shared
The love we did share
Will fly with me in the winds

10:30 am
July 4, 1993
Block 84, Flat 3
QAU Summit Quarters (Comoros)
Asokoro District
Abuja

WHEN GIRLS FALL IN LOVE, THEY SOLILOQUISE

Young Mr. Romeo
Your long letter
Has just arrived
I wish to let you know
That I am convinced
That I am too young
Just too young to love
Too young to fall in love
Too young to bare my heart
10   Too young to explore your mind
For my academic ambitions
Must always come first
For I want to be a doctor
For I want to be great
To be a great woman
Just like any man
For now I am in love
Not with your heart
Rather with my ambition
20   I am scared of your love
For Daddy has my love
For Mum too knows
For Mum too feels
For Mum sees me
As her super baby
Who will trail the pages
The rough pages of books

Not just any book
Not just any simple book
30   But the big, big books
The medical books
Which explore the human anatomy
Which teach us how to save lives
Which makes us noble women
For Mum wants me to read
To read these great books
To bring back home many glories
Yes, many glories to glow
To glow in her heart
40   As a befitting reward
A noble reward for her
For her suffering
For her long restlessness
For her breast milk
For she toiled for me
For all her love
For being so nice
For caring so much
To bring me into the world
50   She will not be happy with me
If I fall in love with you
If I fall in love now
Your love will dampen my ambition
Your love, Mr. Romeo
I must not return your love
Maybe if not now
Maybe later
When my dreams have come true
60   And my mum has seen her dreams
When my mum has seen me through
Through the rough battle ahead
The battle I have heard
The sleepless battle
The battle fought

Only within the four walls
Of the university
For when I have fought
And won the battle
70   I could then start loving
You, Master Romeo
I must not tell you my heart
I must not let loose the feeling
That haunts my virgin heart
For Dad loves me very much
For Dad will be jealous
Dad will be jealous of you
For he loves me too much
For he takes me along
80   When he goes on long trips
For he watches when I sleep
For he strokes my hair
When he is in a good mood
Dad will kill you, Mr. Romeo
He does not want anyone
Any young man, any Romeo
To steal me away from him
For when he wants to call me
He forgets my name
90   And yells out, "Nma!"
Which means beauty?
Being the only girl of the house
I answer my dad's call
In anticipation that he calls me
Young Mr. Romeo
You must learn to bear
For I know I love you dearly
For just what you are for the man in you
For the youth in your heart
100   For the love in your heart
For your unrivalled peculiarities
Mr. Romeo, my Romeo

"Oh, what did I say?
Suppose he was here
Here in my room
Let's face it squarely
Don't I love him?
Is he not My Romeo?
But I must not let him know
110   I must keep the secret
Only to myself
Only to my heart
Only to the four walls
Of my room
My lonesome room
Oh! But they say
The walls do have ears?
No, no one else must know
That I am in love
120   With Mr. Romeo
I must play the game tough
Very tough with him
He must fall on his knees
To get to my love
He must learn to fill
All the leaves of grass
In the love forest
With poems of love
He must learn to endure
130   All that it takes
To win my heart
For I have promised
Mum and Dad to excel
To exploit the thoughts of men
To explore the pages of books
The knowledge of great men
To build on my own intellect
To a level close to Romeo's
For I know he is a gifted guy

140	I swore never to tell him
	My mind, my heart, my love
	My love for him
	For I dream of my Romeo
	My great Knight
	My great conqueror
	Conqueror of many lands
	In his white powerful horse
	Coming back home victoriously
	To find me trapped
150	On the roof of a castle
	By his enemies
	Then catching sight of me
	He galloped home
	And climbed to the castle top
	To rescue me
	With Jimmy his Stallion
	Staring at us on the roof
	He came to the top to rescue me
	From the troubles
160	From the burden
	Of my academic ambitions
	For I know what I want
	I also know one thing
	That I am in love
	I am in love with Romeo
	With Mr. Romeo
	No, not Mr. Romeo
	Not Mr. Romeo anymore
	I should call him My Romeo
170	Yes! Really *my Romeo*
	For I know I may be young
	But I am nineteen
	I may be very ambitious
	For despite my great ambition
	For despite my late teen age
	I am in love with Romeo

For I am certain that Romeo
Will give me a helping hand
To realize my great ambition
180   My long cherished ambition
For I know deep down me
That I need someone
Someone who cares
Someone who appreciates
Someone who cares like Romeo
For I need somebody to care
Somebody to love and care for me
Somebody to love me
Somebody to care for me
190   Somebody to write poems for me
Somebody to call me his princess
Though I must not be cheap
He has to work for it
As much as galloping
And climbing to the castle top
To rescue his princess
Now his heart, his queen
And then take me home
In his white stallion
200   To Mum and Dad
Yes, to Mum and Dad
Who will be very proud
Who will be really proud
Very proud of Romeo
Who will protect me
Long after they have lived
Then he will give me
A new name to match
He will call me Juliet
210   And we would have fulfilled
The great legend of William Shakespeare"
Where the legendary Romeo died
With his Juliet in his arms

For us we will live
We will live on and on
Here and ever after.

6:00 pm
July 20, 1993
Kubwa
Abuja

Too Young To Love

I was awakened from bed like other days
By the brilliant, harsh, and innocent sun rays
Peeping through my window without blinds
My head was filled with the thoughts of you
Your name filled my mouth
Your thoughts ached in my head
Your long neglect did not help
For you have abandoned me helplessly
To the mercy of the winds of time
10   For last night I hugged my pillow
Many a time thinking it was you
And my mind tells me that something
Unknown to my innocent heart
Something I do not know may be on my way
Something I cannot predict may stop me
From reaching the heart of my love
For I quizzed myself many more times
Than my little brain could recall
What on this earth could be the unknown?
20   Why you have refused to write me?
Why you have refused to ask about me?
Why you despise me so much as to hate?
Why you no longer remember me like before?
Why you have refused to return my love?
For who on earth may be stealing your heart?
For who on earth may be standing on our love path?
For who on earth may be distorting the aura?
Of love linking you and me on our memory lane
And one thought seems to have an upper hand

30   Tutoring my little brain about many things
      Maybe you are too young to understand
      Maybe you are too young to fall in love
      Maybe you are shy to say you love me too
      Maybe you feel am standing on your way
      To fulfill your long academic ambitions
      Maybe you are in love with someone else
      Maybe someone has stolen your heart
      Maybe you could never really love
      Maybe you don't have a heart
40   Maybe you were never told about love
      Maybe you are too innocent to fall in love
      Maybe you are shy to love
      Maybe you are too young to love
      Maybe you are scared of what mum will say
      Maybe you are just your daddy's pet
      Maybe am too plebeian for your royal hands
      Maybe you are scared about what people will say
      Maybe you could never really love me
      Maybe virgin girls like you
50   Leave your heads in the clouds
      And your innocent hearts in the green Kubwa Hills
      Such that young men toil day in and out
      In search of this innocent love proof heart
      And they scramble to bow just to kiss your toes
      And your head swells in innocence and pride
      And you are never ruffled to utter a word
      For your head is full of pride and preoccupied
      With your great virtues and prize of womanhood
      Which seem to spill from yourself
60   For my heart has cried many times
      In anticipation, how you could read my mind
      To return the innocence and purity of love
      That flows out from my heart every day
      Like the living waters from Ezeiyi fountains
      Bubbling pure and spotlessly clean to nobles
      And to the humble plebeians who parch in thirst
      For to cry everyday to the rays of the sun

In supplication, that I am greatly in love
May never change the course of the wind
70   For the centerpiece of my love is you
For I have cried and searched unendingly for you
But all has been in vain, and my daily pleads
Seem to bore the nerve fibers in my brain
For my efforts to tell the world again and again
About my enduring elusive love
I seem to have lost grips with the wind
For every other day I keep asking myself
Suppose she wakes up one bright Harmattan morning
Picks up her pen to say she never loved me
80   Then what will I do with my petals of rose
Then one thought told me that it would be a relief
For then, I could go home and stop brooding
I could pour myself a little Irish cream
To celebrate my eventual liberation from bondage
For how much I could love has caged me in prison
Where no one else could render any help
Except your immortal innocent heart
For then I could go home to make amends
For I could make amends where need be
90   And leave the rest for the winds to fix
For though I could try consoling myself
But I know deep down me I have lost
One great battle in my life goals
The battle to win your virgin heart
And if then I should have a daughter
Whose mother is the wind
I will give her your name—Nma
For even then I will always love you
As I have always done in the spirit
100   For my love for you is beyond the flesh
For it is a love that is born and nurtured
In the winds of the spirit world
It is a love of purity
It is a love of absolute dedication
It is a love of innocence at heart

It is a love not built on infatuation
It is a natural kind of love
It is an obsessive and crazy kind of love
It is a consuming love
110 An intoxicating love
A love devoid of jealousy
It is the peak of the purity of love
It is a love without a heart
An unassuming and unreserved kind of love
It is a rare kind of love
A love born and nurtured in innocence
It is a genuine kind of love
A love as pure as a dove
A love as innocent as the clouds
120 A love as gentle as raindrops
A love as peaceful as the Lilies
A love born in spirit without flesh
An unequalled kind of love
A love which could never be matched
For the craze of my love for you
For the dedication of my love for you
For the power behind my love for you
For the purity and innocence behind my love for you
Could stir the hills and the Tibetan mountains
130 To dance to the tune of my endless rhymes
For silver and gold have I not
But all I have to give is love
The kind of love that spills from a heart
The kind of love that echoes from the green Kubwa Hills
The kind of love that flows like the river Niger
The kind of love that glitters like gold
The kind of love that comes from the heart
The kind of love that flows from my pen
The kind of love that gives me sleepless nights
140 The kind of love that makes me crazy
An unending and overwhelming kind of love
A kind of love that is beyond explanation
A kind of love that makes me drunk

Even when I abhor alcoholic beverages
A love borne from the purity of the mind
A love that spills from an immaculate heart
A love, an unreserved love of a kind
For the love of the flesh has no nidus
For the love of beauty has no limit
150   For the love of wealth never really lasts
For the love of glamour passes with the winds
For the love of materialism is vanity
For the love of money in insatiable
But the purity of though in your heart
The purity and innocence of the virgin in you
Spills out to me in evocation
Pouring down the virgin scenes of green Kubwa Hills
Where my spirit has married the muse
160   Of your innocence and virgin heart
For your snow-white youthful heart
Could wake the dead from their graves
For the uncontaminated youthful thoughts in your heart
Lights a love candle flame which burns endlessly
Throwing more light and skill into my fountain pen
Pouring down like rain from my little head
For even if you come out tomorrow
To deny ever knowing my name
I am not the least ashamed of course
170   For to love from the purity of innocence
Is to love like a child a love without blemish
For my love for you is a love without blemish
For the inspirations which you have evoked
Fall cats and dogs in this unique panorama
Of the crescent green Kubwa Hills
Which has engulfed me in its torrential waves
For the unequalled evocation from your immaculate heart
Has formed dew drops on top of the green Kubwa Hills
For on top of the green Kubwa Hills east of the crescent
180   Are virgin girls born
And in the east of the green Kubwa Hills
They grow from a heart without blemish

Before maturity and age brought by the winds of time
Throws the virgin girls aboard—the West of green Kubwa Hills
Where men and the evils men do
To the purity of virgin hearts abound
For though you are too young to understand
For though you are too young to love
But the truth remains that your innocence
190   And the purity of thought in your heart
Is a product of the time machine
Which only requires the gradual movement
Of the restless hands of the clock
To become a piece of history on pages of books
For time makes things pure and innocent
For time also labors things unholy and sinful
For your youth and the purity of your heart
Is the only weapon your heart has now
To spill out what it does to the evocation
200   Of innocence and purity which forms early morning clouds
Top of the east of the panoramic green Kubwa Hills
Caressing my lovesick heart endlessly
In a total submission to an unreserved love
Begging the queen of the green Kubwa Hills
Hoping that one day you will be mine.

6:30 pm
December 24, 1994
Abuja Clinics Limited
Karu FHA Estate
Abuja

IMAGES OF LOVE

Love is an incredible phenomenon
Of the rarest existing species
The products of this special breed
Are always young
They never grow old
They are always young
They never grow old as should be
Love, the seed of love
Once sowed even in the worst soil
10   Germinates even with the least moisture
It endures all hardships
To uphold herself
Even in the angry sea
She asserts her endurance
Sometimes from the thin air
Where we get the breath of life
Sometimes from the passing wind
Which blows across to brighten our day
Blowing her hair forward and backward
20   Sometimes from the whiteness of her teeth
Which leaves a snowy glow flash bye
Sometimes from her large eyeballs
Which harbor the great queen called Love
Making his heart beat a little faster
Than it always does
Enduring with the least trivial
Love endures even for his height
Looking down her head
In a ballroom dance

30   Love grows even
From this gentle voice
Echoing behind a feminine touch
Ringing out like church bells
Warming to joyful happy glows
Coming from the inner minds
Striking an enduring cord
That grows on and on
Growing and glowing as love always does
Sometimes from her graceful steps
40   Sometimes from her bluntness
Carrying with it the true image
Yes, the true picture of life
Which endures the tricks of time
Sometimes from his cooing speech
That seems to melt the honey pot
In the attempt of winning a heart
Sometimes from the dimples on her cheek
Leaving a print mark of uniqueness
Making her obviously distinct
50   In the teeming crowd
Sometimes from her magnetic beauty
For he dreams of the angels
Which will emerge
As the offspring of her endeavors
Bringing into the world
These rare species
Who may have been made
The day God opted for rest
After his long hours of creation
60   Sometimes sad enough
From the obvious wealth magnet
Which forms the focus of her dreams
The pivot of her imaginations
Maybe to escape
From poverty shackles
Which lasts as long
As the wealth endures

Fading faster into twilight
Than its unusual exit
70 For it has no moisture
No soil at all
To survive and endure,
For it was never sowed
Many times from the beauty
Of her black long hair
For it leaves the memories
Of princesses and queens
Who adore our exotic movies
Painting life as roses without thorns
80 Giving man this image of a mere robot
Living a life as mechanical as the clock
Sometimes from his manifestation of ingenuity
This marks him out as outstanding
For she dreams of a seed
So generously and greatly endowed
With the flavor of superior genes
Carrying the genes of great men
Unfolding the roots of great women
Who will make their great marks
90 In our world of greater tomorrow
Making the world a better place
Leaving footprints
In the enduring sands of time

1:20 am
July 18, 1994
Gwagwalada Crescent
Phase II Site I
Kubwa, Abuja

Ode To Nma: Never Love A Teenage Girl

Once upon a time
In the country Hills of Eluama
I met a virgin teenage elegant daughter
That was in her home with her Mum and Dad
It was her junior brother's birthday
Then she was so young with an innocent face
Then I fell in love with her in her home
She is the ideal of my great imaginations
She is as bright as the morning sun
10   She is as pretty and as good as a goose
She is a rare gem from a nicety mine
Her skin is as beautiful as my petals of rose
Her hair is as dark and as long as ever
Her face is as beautiful and as round
And as smooth and as good as Paducah apple
Her innocent voice rings out like a violin
And her finger pulps are as soft and as tender
As anything as good as love herself can be
Her strides are as regal and as graceful
20   As anything as good as love
And her intellect as good as beauty and brains
Her worth is as great as the golden geese
And as such I presumed that she could only lay
Golden eggs as good as the geese
Then I embarked on a troubled voyage
To explore the unknown and untapped virgin jungle
Then I wrote her a letter at school
And she did reply on time with hesitation

She was as innocent as a lamb in her language
30   The innocence and purity in her heart
Was as palpable as a hypertensive radial pulse
Then before anyone could say Cha-Klo-Gba!
I fell in love again and again and again
With the goose yet to lay her golden eggs
I got carried away into the world
Of the unknown full of assumptions
Then I dreamt dreams about her in my arms
I dreamt dreams about her on my bed
I dreamt dreams about her in my dining
40   Great dreams indeed that she is the mother
The inspirational mother of my babies
My babies who will be born genius
My kids who will be super babies
I comforted myself in my dreams
That from the great genes of their mother
The super gene pool of the golden geese
My offspring will be born into greatness
Then I fell in love first with my head
Then my hands, my legs, my chest
50   And then my aching lovesick heart
Then I was swimming in a pool
Bubbling with too many uncertainties
Assumptions, yes, unimaginable assumptions
Assumptions which could roast a man's heart
Then my very close friend observed
That I am paying an undue attention
To a virgin teenage girl of all eves
And he sounded the alarm without mincing words
"Never fall in love with a teenage girl
60   Never love a teenage girl
She could break your delicate lovesick heart
They are very temperamental
They are very unpredictable
You are indeed playing with a time bomb
When it explodes, you have yourself to blame
You better be careful

Or you could regret that you ever did
You could withdraw before it's too late"
To my friend's assumptions it was still early
70   But the untold truth, but now an open secret
To my innocent and helpless lovesick heart
Is that I was too late to imagine
Then my head started pounding
Like a pile driver
Then my head was aching
Then my mind was sick
Then I was really scared
For I questioned myself many times
"How could you feel if she never
80   Accepted the favor to wear your rings"
I found myself sweating profusely
In the serenity of the moonlight
Where I have gone to meditate
About the only love in my heart
For then I had fallen greatly in love
For then my heartbreak started
There in my friend's house
That same day he did warn me
My fears reached the innocent white clouds
90   For fear that my dreams and imaginations
May never crystallize into a reality
For then I had written her a sonnet
A creation I called my own masterpiece
Pouring my heart down in full
Like Mother Nature wets our soil
When she is full with tears of joy
Then I gave the sonnet to an artist to paint
After which he could write out the piece
With gold ink to express my heart
100   Then he could frame it with a silver frame
Then it was to be a birthday gift
To my heart, my teenage girl
But when my friend saw it in display
He did not hesitate to sound the alarm

Then when I wrote my teenage girl
To inquire about her genotype
She replied me in a very temperamental language
She lost her head and her good manners
In the quick anticipation of my moves
110 My preparations to clear the grounds well enough
To see the way clearly to bring my calabash of palm wine
Then she was mad with me for daring
To walk on the surface where the angels
Yes, where the angels fear to tread
She chastised me in full in strong anticipation
Of my endless dreams to bring her close
To bring her closest to my right atrium
She probably swore never to write me again
She even despised me to the point of hate
120 Meanwhile, many girls are praying day and night
For any man at all to know their genotype
Many thousands of them are roaming the streets
Searching and searching for their heart desire
Then I wrote my teenage virgin princess of Eluama
I gave her a lot of reasons for my demand
I pleaded with her to forgive me
I begged and begged a teenage girl
Like I have never begged any girl in my life
Rather the sight of me nauseated her much
130 She never wanted to see me again
She hated me, she despised me
I appealed to her immortal heart
In several ways to appease the gods
But like a teenage virgin girl which she is
She blocked her ears with cotton wool
And set my long love letters ablaze
I bought her cards wishing her success
I bought her cards wishing her Merry Christmas
I sent her cards endeared with love poems
140 I sent her cards that sang valentine songs
I sent her cards that hum the Christmas carol
I bought her a necklace made of colored beads

I bought her bangles made of quartz stones
I sent her bangles made of elephant tusks
I asked her to forgive me
I lay on my lonely bed and cried all night long
Stood in front of my standing mirror
Talking to myself, pretending it was her
I hoped that somehow by telepathy
150   She could read the agony and grief
Yes, the pains and despair in my heart
But none ever moved her
She never wrote me again
Then she haunted me all the time
I remembered her each time
I saw a round faced fair girl
For her skin is as fair as the day
I knelt down before my mirror
Begging her on the other side
160   I saw myself kneeling down
I saw myself shedding tears
I could not believe it was me
I pitied my poor innocent heart
I felt very sorry for myself
As I never could tell what is happening to me
What exactly that is passing through me
I could never believe myself
For all these craze in the name of love
I prayed to God many times to give her to me
170   I painted her whole self in my poems
I saw her in the setting sun
Sometimes I beheld her in the rising sun
She is abundantly manifest in the raindrops
The birds many times sang songs
Unknown to them with her sweet name
There at the peak of the green Kubwa Hills
For many times I climbed to the top
And sat down on the leaves of grass
I meditated fruitlessly listening in the dark
180   Listening to a voice that may come in the dark

Listening to a call in the dark
Listening to hear her call my name
In the stillness of the quiet night
Listening to a sweet voice which could be hers
Her voice calling out my name
I woke up from bed with the thought of her
I sang endless songs with her name
She captured my whole being in love
She gave me her fishing hook to swallow
190   With a false love bait dangling from it
Then I pleaded to the moon to shine
I pleaded with the sun to set
I pleaded for night to come
So that I could fall asleep for a while
To forget the intoxication of her love
But none could rescue me
And I found my helpless self
Struggling and battling from the task
That task of love I gave myself
200   The task of an endless love I gave myself
The heavy burden of love not returned
Then I went on a voyage across many lands
I went on a voyage across many rivers
I went on a voyage across many hills
I went on a voyage across many mountains
I went on a voyage across many seas
Where the goddess of love
Lives in her blue mansions
Then I fulfilled the necessary rituals
210   Before I could behold her royal majesty
Venus, the goddess of love and beauty
When Venus appeared from the blue sea
She looked at my heavy heart
She saw the amount of love in my heart
She witnessed the task and adventure
Through sleepless nights and emptiness
As she looked at me closer and closer
She was grieving with tears

Yes, tears were pouring out from her eyes
220   She admired the courage in my heart
She admired the great love in my heart
She admired the purity and innocence of my love
She was moved with great pity
Because she confessed to me
That there was virtually nothing
Absolutely nothing that she could do
She felt pity for my lonesome lovesick heart
She felt for me with a lot of emotions
She felt for me with some compassion
230   Then she told me that I should not despair
That the teenage girl my heart is after
Is not for me in our mortal world
In our world of flesh and blood
Then she asked me to make some atonements
To appease the heart of my teenage princess
Whom my whole innocent heart is after
There and then I made my atonements
Indeed without delay in a record time
She was marveled at my dexterity
240   Then she asked me to go home
That my real love will find my lovesick heart
Then I went home to find that my girl
My virgin princess of Eluama
The unrivalled Beauty that grows
Only on the hills and the plains of Eluama
The elegant daughter of Eluama
The core focus of my endless inspirations
That my love has abandoned me in the cold
And went on a lonesome train journey
250   That she sort for me when I was away
She looked for me when I went to see Venus
Then she never saw me again
For someone told her that I have drowned
That I am no more there to love her
Then she cried like she never did
Then she sat down without food

For seven whole days and nights
Reading all the poems of love
That she inspired me to write
260   Then at the end her heart was heavy
And she then abandoned me in ignorance
Believing the JONES that I had drowned
Then she went on a train journey
To an unknown land of the gypsies
My heart ached and ached every day
My mind was at the doorstep
Hoping against hope in the earnest faith
That one day my love will come back
That my love will come back to me
270   So that we could live in our home
The Lilies, which I built for us
Just for the two of us
For then I sent the kites
For then I sent the wind
For then I sent the innocent doves
For then I sent the power eagle
To reach the unknown land
Where my love has been
To tell her that she should come home
280   To tell her that I am still waiting
That I am still faithfully waiting for her
Then I remembered what my friend told me
"Never fall in love with a teenage girl
Never love a teenage girl"
For then I needed not be told
That my lovesick heart
Has fallen into bits and pieces
Though I sit there smiling all day
Pretending that all is well with me
290   When actually I have lost one great battle
A battle greater than the loss of Waterloo
For Napoleon went with his heart intact
To St. Helena Island where he died
But my own heart eluded me

For she has gone on a train journey
For she has gone on an endless trip
An endless train journey
Where not even my friends that I sent—
The winds, the kites, the doves and the power eagles
300   Could reach her to deliver my message
For then I am learning my lesson
In a very hard way
Never to fall in love
With a virgin teenage girl

2:10 am
January 12, 1994
Abuja Clinics
Garki, Abuja

NATURE IS ROMANTIC

Take a look at the snowcapped Kilimanjaro
Standing in the Kenyan border like a Pajero
Behold the great waters of Victoria Falls
Watch the angry sea build her walls
Erect her great fragile mansions
And even demolish them in her fashions
Take a quick cover from the wind's form
Save your skin from the desert sand storm
On your honeymoon trip to Gao
10   Where winds build their sands below
Watch the busy ants go in and out
With their wares from their pinholes without
See the rose buds blossom in the rains
Take a look as the water lily entertains
Smiling broadly to the rising sun
Have you ever seen the army of ants run
Have you taken a time off to visit
The virgin jungles of Africa in transit
And listen to the birds sing their rhymes
20   Listen to the jungle night talk in their chimes
Tell us the tempo, the tunes of their voices
As she savors your ears in her own choices
In the great flavor of nature's romance
Take your time and watch the spider dance
To catch her prey in her usual instinctive exploits
Look up and behold in the sky the great flights
Of the Albatross migrating instinctively to warmer lands
When birds listen to and obey nature's commands
Have you ever listened to the ripples

30   From a brook falling over a rapid of dimples

Taking your better half along with your group
Embark on a camping trip with your troop
Then write her a line or two in good rhymes
To brighten her day in swinging ringo styles
Take your time and open your lungs
In a healthy laughter when you can
It adds more being to your life
Take a walk to the lonesome park
Allow yourself a lone moment
And look up into the sanity
Of the scenic blue sky
Allowing you to fly off like a dove
Soaring with the moving clouded head
Have you ever paused for a good while?
To commune with the glory of the setting sun
Now wait a minute!
And behold the splendor of the rising sun
Have you observed the human face?
Of the enigmatic Zuma Rock
Staring indifferently at your wondering eyes
Take a holiday to the Swiss Alps
See for yourself the beauty of snow
Echoing the wonders and greatness
Of the living mighty hands of God
Visit the flower gardens in the spring
Watch the butterflies move
From one flower to another
Watch the bees as they steal
The nectar from the flower for honey
Helping them pollinate their mates
And there are no policemen to arrest them
Listen to the brown African doves
As they sing and coo along
Always in a happy pair
With their clean and immaculate hearts
They never flirt like humans do

Take some time off to an African village
Perhaps Eluama if you choose to
Watch the native chickens protect their young
From the charging angry hawks
Watch the winds kiss the leaves
Making the trees to bow
Reluctantly in condescending homage
As the innocent winds pass across
To pacify the human nature
Look up again into the clouds
Watch their puppies run for a date
Where they hug and kiss
Their loved ones
Shedding the tears of love
Falling to us here as rain
What can you really say?
The power behind all these:
The wonders of the human eye
Have you paused to think about it?
It is really something else
Indeed some great perceptions
For nature is splendidly romantic

9:30 pm
July 15, 1993
Gwagwalada Crescent
Yaba Street 'E' Close,
Phase II, Site I,
Kubwa, Abuja

TELL NMA

Please tell NMA that am weeping
That tears are dropping down my eyes
Not because am not manly enough
Not because she is the only girl in the world
Not because I cannot get another girl
For too many girls here are falling over
Begging me to give them a minute attention
But I have told them the truth, the bitter truth
That I am in love with NMA
10   For she has stolen my heart
And given it to the goddess of love
To keep it safe for her when she is ready
But meanwhile she does not give me attention
Tell NMA
That 'am fine here, though very lonely
Tell her that today is Christmas day
That I am singing alone in my house
That I have been expecting a Christmas card
That none from her has come my way
20   Tell NMA
That my life is empty and lonesome
For my thoughts, my actions, my emotions
Are all in limbo waiting patiently
For I woke up from bed this morning
With thoughts of her making me sad
As I could not go to Eluama for Christmas
Then I suddenly found myself standing
Before the mirror and talking to her
"I have just come to see you and only you

30	Please do not run away anymore
	For how long are you going to continue running?
	I have come to ask you why all these troubles?
	I want to know what you think about me
	Please tell me everything, do not be afraid
	If you don't love me, don't feel scared
	To say so, for sometimes we may never love
	All those who may have affection for us
	For you to hide under the canopy of being young
	Is not enough excuse for you to kill one heart
40	For I wish to tell you that all is well
	You need not bother too much
	For I wish you well in all your endeavors
	For I cherish the zeal to succeed in your heart
	For I share your dreams with you wholly
	Though I wish to tell you to be careful
	For I cannot stand to hear any ugly stories
	You must learn to be a wall made of rock
	You must not allow yourself to be deceived
	For the bad boys are everywhere
50	For the Casanovas are lurking around the corners
	You must stand firm to protect you pride
	The priceless aura of womanhood in you
	For you must learn to be like the Shulamite
	For you must learn to love like a child
	For you must learn to uphold the great virtues
	The impeccable gem of every single woman
	For I cannot live to hear that you are spoilt
	For I will wage war against any man who dares
	For I will fight in defense to protect your virtues
60	For the honor of a virgin princess of Eluama
	Is the worthiest dowry that a man could pay
	To win the heart of an elegant daughter of the hills
	For many times I have stood like this brooding
	Talking to myself, pleading for you to understand
	That I do not mean any harm at all
	That my only problem is that I am in love
	That I am madly in love with my heart

Instead of my head, and you are not moved
You have to try to understand me now
70 Because I will not always be around
For you need to return my love
So that you could have something to keep
For me, when am away to Timbuktu
In search of the treasures in the Sudan
For the adventures to the Treasure Island
Requires the good wishes from a loved one
For you have to stand to say good-bye
For you have to stand on my side
For I need your priceless moral support
80 For I need your love to spur me on
To greater heights to overcome all odds
For I need your good wishes in my adventures
For your name has always brought good luck
To my lovesick and innocent heart
For you may be as young as a lamb
Remember tomorrow you will become a sheep
You need a caring hand of love
To show you around with tender loving care
You need a hand that understands what is love
90 You need a hand as loving and as tender as mine
For you could explore the love market
With the rarest piece of gemstone mine
Full of excitements, adventures and fun
Though you need a guide to show you through
But beware of vampires who rupture the hymen
For they abound in their thousands every where
For they are sweet tongued and lie proofed
For they are fake and unreal in all senses
They tell you lies and confuse your little brain
100 But though in the course of the search for love
The search for our ideal man and woman
We have many times fallen into the wrong hands
For you must learn that there is no ideal man
For you must learn that there is no ideal woman
For all that, are fantasies of growth

Which clear from our heads like a mirage
At the point we leave the university campus
At the point we are thrown into the world
Into the intricate harsh world
110   Full of men and women vampires
Who thrive on the young blood of boys and girls
For I want to reassure you that I am here
I am extending my innocent hand of love
A hand of love which no money can buy
A hand of love which no one else has got
A helping hand of love, a tender loving care
A hand of love to serve as a guide
As you explore the world around you
A true hand of love to keep and cherish
120   A hand of love of innocence without blemish
A hand of love as pure and as immaculate
As your spotless virgin heart in the brew
For though the tears of love are falling endlessly
From my eyes all this while as I talk
It is not the tear of weakness on the part of my manliness
But it is a tear of love not returned
Heavy and troubled tears of love not returned
For my emotions have long been tethered in retrospect
For I cry every morning for you
130   For I will give all I have to hold your hands
For I will grow wings and fly
To see the beauty and innocence in your face
For I will send a present to the moon
For you to call me dear for real
For I will bribe the sun to set early
So that the gentle moon could appear
And we can hold hands all night
And caress the thoughts and feelings from the moonlighting
For if you vow to love me in the moonlighting
140   Then I will swear to the moon to drink nowhere
Except from your refreshing spring of charm
Which has haunted my youthful heart
In an unprecedented and overwhelming love shuttle

For to say less will amount to my dying in silence
But I have refused to die in silence

Without letting my feelings known to the world
For to love is one thing,
But love not returned is yet another
As such I plead with you to tell me your mind
150   You need not feel pity for breaking my heart
Could it be that you don't love me too
Do not feel scared to tell me so
Do not feel sorry for me though
For it is all my fault for falling in love
Not with humans with flesh and blood
But with the serenity and panorama
Of the green Kubwa Hills
Harbored in your virgin eyeballs
For the scenes in your heart
160   The topography of your contours
The beauty of your enduring vegetation
And the charm of your great features
Have enslaved my poor self
In obsession and supplication to point of perfection
For anyone may think am frank crazy
But the truth remains with me
The love of home, the beauty of Eluama
The charm of that little town on hills
The unending growing nostalgia of Adaoma Hills
170   Will haunt my thoughts and the inspirations
Unendingly all the days of my mortal life
For my inexhaustible love for Eluama
Could never reach a climax
For you have epitomized the core feelings
That flow from my heart to our home
For I do not know what to do
For I am not ashamed of my love
For Eluama has married the muse in my heart
And decided to crystallize it on top
180   Of the virgin scenes of the crescent green Kubwa Hills

Which spur my inspirations every moment of the day
For you have served as the vehicle
An instrument of focus to reality
Of the great torrential down pour
Which has long been wetting my cheeks
Making me cry every day in endless love
In an untold love not returned
A true love to an innocent virgin girl
Who out of purity and innocence of age
190   Has shied away from my endless pleas
My endless pleads to be loved from the heart
For my pillow is wet with my tears
When it dawned on me that it was not you
That I was talking to myself in the mirror
That you are hundreds of miles away in Eluama
Entertaining your family guests at home
While I savor the pains of love not returned
Refusing to go out and see anyone
Though it is a Christmas day of all days"

10:45 am
December 25, 1993
Abuja Clinics Ltd.
Karu, Abuja

TAKE A MESSAGE TO NMA

Take a message to Nma
Tell her that the clouds invited me
Top of the east of green Kubwa Hills
Informing me that the queen of the hills
Wants to have a chat with me
In the thick of the descending clouds
That the aim of the invitation is for me
To behold the pulsatile beauty in my heart—Nma
That while I am coming I should be prepared
10   That there may be a need for a sacrifice
For the queen of the east of green Kubwa Hills
Never invites men to the haven of virgin girls
But when she has to, the man is transformed
Into the innocence and purity of the clouds,
Tell Nma that when I labored to the peak
Of the panoramic crescent green Kubwa Hills
I saw great things in answer to this queen's invitation
That on my way I saw too white doves
Cooing to each other like acts in love parks
20   That the leaves of grass were smiling at me
That the petals of rose where falling out
As a welcome sign to my unannounced visit
That the winds of time stood for a while
While the innocent ripples of the brooks of green Kubwa Hills
Bubbled away in sincere greeting to my arrival
As they labored through their narrow beds to the east of Eden
Where the first pair of human virgins made by
The great hands of God once lived without sin
That the ants were singing aloud to my hearing

30	And the rocks were sparkling green
	While the bark of trees scratched my lonesome back
	That my journey up to the peak of green Kubwa Hills
	Was very lonesome without much fun
	But as I was going in frank anticipation to behold
	Her innocent pretty face, I took much delight
	In the spring time of nature standing on my way
	That my heart was beating fast in great anticipation
	As I got closer and closer to the peak
	As I neared the foot of the clouds
40	On the top of the crescent green Kubwa Hills
	A basin of dew drops poured over me
	Like a shower of blessings from above
	And as I got to the door of the white clouds
	I announced my presence with humility
	Then I was told that I have to make some atonements
	In the form of some creative verse of sort
	For I had earlier been warned to be prepared
	Then I asked the people of the clouds
	For a moment of quietude for me to marry
50	The great muse that flows like an innocent stream
	At the peak of the panoramic green Kubwa Hills
	For there at the top of these innocent green Hills
	I looked down to mother earth in admiration
	Here if I dare raise my hands up
	I will touch the serene quiet clouds
	Here if I open my mouth I could
	Converse with the angels in the heavens
	Here if I go into deep meditation
	God's hand could be seen sticking out
60	Here the beauty of the earth in virgin scenes
	Is at an enduring peace with herself
	For nature here decided to have her bath nude
	Such that I could behold her intricate curves
	Running through beautiful contours in truncation
	From here I saw the great nude of Abuja
	As nature had made her and left her long ago
	Here I could see a great plateau of a landscape

Which over the centuries has had a bath severally
By the powerful agents of denudation
70   Truncating the plateau in a unique fashion
Into hills, plains, valleys, and lowlands
For the serene topography is clothed green
With myriad pockets of human activity
Running through the expressways and settlements
The roads meander in intricate fashions
And some of the buildings stick out like fingers
Which are endlessly pointing to the sky
Seeming to ask God to come down quick
To save the dying human race from a catastrophe
80   Which seem imminent, starting probably from here
From here around my foot, the rocks were happy
The leaves of grass were joyful and at ease
Even the wind was kissing my petals of rose
As the clouds were rapt watching me in isolation
Drifting away in my own muse shuttle
Which takes only one astronaut at a time
To its own outer space to endless explorations
Here my mind was blue and green
My pulse had been racing like in an Olympiad
90   My thoughts were full of anticipations for a surprise
As I explored the vastness of these inspiring hills
For the hills themselves have hearts and thoughts
For the hills themselves have limbs and faces
For the hills are even as humane as are humans
For the hills allow the grass to grow with joy
For the hills allow the petals of rose to smile at me
For the hills are virgins and innocent
Such that they invite the holy doves
To mate on their tops even close to the clouds
100   For the hills are kind and generous at heart
For the hills even care to lend a hand
To dissipate the youthful energies that build
Explosively in the minds of the youth which flow
In an endless inspiration as muse to the brain
For the hills are endlessly in love to all

For the clouds themselves have refused to be isolated
For the clouds have stretched a hand of invitation
To us mortals to pay them a visit
Even asking us for a return for a date
110   For I have longed for a date with Nma
For I have asked the clouds to help me out
For the queen of the crescent green Kubwa Hills
Have opted to act as a mediator
To bridge the endless gap between me
And my endless love in the blinds
At the other side of green Kubwa Hills
Where maybe a love candle burns
On and on and never goes off
While we mortals endlessly seek for muse
120   On this side where the love candle is rare
Where the efforts to light a love candle flame
Of an endless love drives a young man crazy
As he pines for a time which may never come
For now the task has been completed
And I handed it over to the clouds
But the queen of the panoramic green Kubwa Hills
Sends another message across that she is sorry
That I cannot see my heartthrob today
That she is busy in the beauty rooms
130   That I have to accept another date
For then Nma would have grown stronger and stronger
To stand the current from my fountain pen
For then Nma would have matured to be let out
From the clouds and handed over to the time machine
When I could be allowed to behold her in full

11:30 am
December 26, 1993
Karu, Abuja

TELL MY DEAR MOTHER

Tell my sweet mother
That I am twenty-eight years now
Tell my dear mother
That nobody loves me as she should
Tell my sweet mother
That I am very lonely
As lonely as a stone
As lonely as a stream
Tell my sweet mother
10   That all those I love do not understand
That there is no one to talk to
That there is no one to talk for me
Like she would have done
Tell my dear mother
That I have read the books in and out
That I have fallen deeply in love
Not with any girl as she may assume
But with the pages of many books
Tell my sweet mother
20   That I have tried to love a girl in the past
But she rejected me because I have no money
For my love was pure and innocent
Tell my dear mother
That I have nobody to breastfeed me
When am thirsty and hungry for food
No one to cry to when there is need
Tell my sweet mother
That she should come back to me
And give me all the love

30   That my heart has been craving for
        For I have never been loved since she left me
        Tell my dear mother
        That I have tried to love another girl
        That she is a virgin princess of Eluama
        A teenage elegant daughter of Eluama
        Tell my sweet mother
        That I am in love with the purity and innocence
        From the bottom of my innocent heart
        That the princess does not understand
40   That she pays me back with scorn
        Tell my dear mother
        That life has been not too harsh and not too good
        To my helpless and motherless self
        Tell my sweet mother
        That I am twenty-eight years now
        Yet I am parched for her love—her breast milk
        That I have grown beard
        That I want to get married
        That I am sick sometimes
50   Not because of disease
        But for lack of love and affection
        That I have craved for love
        All my twenty-eight years
        That no love seems to come my way
        Tell my dear mother
        That I am now married to poetry
        That I am in love with the daughter of poetry
        A sweet little teenage girl
        The unrivalled princess of Eluama
60   Whose father is a king
        Tell her that I am in love with the princess from Eluama
        That I want to marry from Eluama
        That Eluama has refused to give me
        Her teenage daughter for a wife
        Tell her that I have tried once
        From the hills in the stone country
        That I failed very badly

That I am trying again—my last chance
Now on a teenage girl
70 Who is very temperamental
And has no love for me
Tell her that I love this girl very much
That her name in our creative world is Nma
That Nma is an elegant daughter of Eluama
Tell my mother
That she should come very quick
She should come very quickly too
To rescue me from the grips
From the power grips of love not returned
80 Tell my sweet mother
That I missed her very greatly
That I have done all I could to Nma
To the teenage elegant daughter
That she does not understand
Tell my dear mother
That I have written Nma
Several long love letters
Pouring my heart down on paper
That I have confessed my endless love
90 All the love in my heart
All the love that flows from my nerves
All the love that spills out from me
Tell my sweet mother
That I have bought a rose flower for Nma
That I have bought her bangles
That I have bought her a brown purse
Spotted with brown paisley designs
With a little mirror to see her pretty face
That I have helped her develop her stamp album
100 That Nma does not seem to understand
That I am really confused and in despair
That I have sent Nma a Christmas card
That I have sent several success cards
All laced with poems of endearment
That some of the cards even sing love songs

While some hum the tunes of Christmas carol
That none have moved her virgin heart
That Nma has refused to return my love
That I am deeply aggrieved and worried
110   Tell my sweet mother
That Nma is not the only virgin in Eluama
That there may be many others I do not know
That the truth remains that I really love her
For my love for Nma has survived
In times of loneliness
In times of happiness
In times of sadness
In times of joy
In times of merriment
120   In times of poetic celebration
When I burn my midnight lamp
Pouring my heart on pages of paper
Hoping they could one day rekindle
A little spot in the minds of the nobles
And that of the plebeians alike
And they could rescue me from my endless love
Tell my dear sweet mother
That I do not know what to do
That I love this girl very much
130   That Nma has refused to reciprocate
My endless love for her
That I know not what to do
That I am really confused
That I am in trouble
That I want to marry from Eluama
Tell my dear mother
That she should come to my rescue
That my heart is heavy for Nma
That she is my last chance at home
140   That if it fails, the gods are to blame
For I have pleaded time and again for them
To give me their daughter for a wife
But they sat there doing very little

While I pine endlessly in isolation
Tell my dear sweet mother
That I have written a book of love
And dedicated it wholeheartedly to Nma
My teenage heartthrob from Eluama
That when I saw the panoramic green Kubwa Hills
150   The virgin scenes of the inspiring green Kubwa Hills
The evocative love jungles of Kubwa Hills
That they inspired great and innocent lines
Flowing innocently from my tireless fountain pen
Tell my dear mother
That the creative aura from the green Kubwa Hills haunts me
That the hills visit my creative aura
Every now and then with high currents
From a great river overflowing its banks
Running toward the east of Eden
160   Tell my mother, my dear sweet mother
That I want to marry Nma
That Nma which means beauty
Is pretty in her own unique way
That Nma is beauty and brains
That Nma is a late teenage girl
Flowing from a river of purity
That Nma does not understand me
That Nma is sick of me
That Nma has refused to love me
170   With the purity and innocence in me
Tell my dear mother
That she should go in the spirit world
And appeal to the goddess of love
And to the spirit of Nma
On my innocent behalf
Tell Venus that I am in love
That she should give me Nma
That she should turn her virgin heart to me
And convince her that I am in love
180   That I am genuinely in love
That I am in love with Nma

That she should not break my heart
That I want to marry her
That I want to marry Nma
That I have seen Nma many times
In my endless dreams of love
That Nma has given me sleepless nights
That Nma could poison my love for her
That my heart is heavy
190   That I do not want to miss her
That I still love the little girl
That she should plead with Nma
Tell my sweet mother
That she should inform Nma
That I miss her very much
The joy of her virgin smiles
The look of her innocent pretty face
The sound of her cooing voice
The romance of walking down the street
200   The great impulse of holding her virgin hands
The glamour of her unique creative beauty
The softness of her flowing African hair
The love of her pure and virgin heart
The dimpled smile on her smooth face
The racing heartbeats of her beautiful heart
The sweet envied talks from her revered company
The pride in me for taking her to our Lilies
The endless inspirations she evokes out of me
Tell my dear mother
210   That if she fails after doing her best
That I will sure carry my calabash of palm wine
To a distant land where humans live in valleys
And in plains instead of the hills as in Eluama
That I could carry my wine to Oshogbo
That I could carry my wine to Omuma
That I could carry my wine to Mbano
That I could carry my wine to Britain
Where people speak through their nostrils
That I could carry my wine to America

220 Where girls love more as they are teenagers
That I could carry my wine to anywhere
To any country that I chose to
That nobody will blame me anymore
For it may seem that I offended the gods
That I wronged the gods from Eluama
That she should endlessly plead with Nma
That she should please consider me
That she should not kill an innocent heart
By refusing my endless pleas for love

11:35 am
January 2, 1994
Abuja Urban Mass Transit
Enugu to Abuja

My Love, My Dreams

When I close my eyes in sleep
I see no one else except you
I see you on my bedside
Your long hair intoxicates me
And my love sapped body cells
For when you smile
The gates of the heavens open
For when you talk
My inner spirit glows
10   For when you sing
My aura duplicates itself
In the attempts to recall
The other me in you
For when you laugh
I hear the swans sing
Waking me up early
From my slumbered sleep
For when you look at me
My whole self melts
20   At the irresistible aura
Of your magnetic beauty
For when you walk
With your graceful strides
I hear your footsteps
Beating in my heart
In your regal and majestic strides
Putting my broken pieces together

Chasing the unkind spirits
Back to the tides
30   For in the brightness of your cheers
The beams of the moon lighting
Make me a lovesick bird
Itching for a walk
In the serene countryside
Embracing the orange
Blessings from the moon
For my heart is restless
And unusually lonesome
In your absence
40   For my whole being is lost
Without you filling
My abandoned empty past
For my dining table is cold
Without your magic touch
For my home is pulseless
Without your crimson heartbeats
Electrifying myself in its aura
For my cup of tea is sour
Without your million dollar smiles
50   For my suit and tie are coarse
Without your usual scrutiny
For my masculine aura is dampened
Without your comforting assurance
For my day at work is dull without humor
Without your good-bye kiss
For my whole life
Is empty and meaningless
Without you to cook my meals
And I keep dreaming on and on
60   For I have come to believe
That life itself is a dream
For first we have to dream dreams
For sometimes our dreams come true

For sometimes our dreams
Never really come true
For we all live in a world of dreams
Man, woman, and child
We all dream dreams
For we must keep dreaming
70   For everything in life
Does begin like a dream
For one thing I do know
Is that you are my dream
Not just my dream
Like I dream every day
But my greatest of all dreams
My life dreams
My dreams to come true
For my dreams of you
80   Is nothing but my life
My real whole life
Let the gods of love
Hear my cries
For I do not wish
To be left in the cold
To be left in the cold anymore
No, not me, not me anymore
No, not anymore
For I do not want to be left
90   In the cold of dreams again for I will cease to dream
Only when my heart stops beating
Abandoning me in the cold of dreams
For my love are my dreams
For the pulsation of my heart
Will rescue me from the endless
Grips and dreams of my love
Drowning my innocent soul
In her chemo-tactic bosom
Leaving me helpless

100   In the cold of my dreams
Till the time she makes
Up her mind to lend me a hand
Of rescue from the dreams of love
The dreams of my endless love

3:40 pm
July 13, 1993
Grace of God Medical Center
Phase II, Site 11
Kubwa, Abuja

Waiting At The Airport

I am here in the airport today
To await your glorious coming
The day is cold and misty
The cloud is foggy like in winter
The sky is heavy and pregnant
The droplets of mist are gathering

The rain in the pregnant clouds
May then decide to fall at will
The visibility is poor for a flight
10 For my lonely heart is cloudy
My eyes are long stretched
As the sun brightens the day again
The cloud cleared after the rain
And I heard a drone in the distance
Before long the big bird appeared
Some distance away in the sky
The drone warms my heart
My imaginations are hovering in the clouds
My troubled pulse is pounding away
20 For I do not know what is amiss
For I could not tell how you are
For I know not even the least
How you are faring far away
Across the blue seas and far beyond
I dream of you in my arms
For too long, I have missed your warmth
For too long, I have not heard your silver voice
Your cooing tunes

That wakes me up from bed
30   Your tender kiss
That lulls me to sleep
Your gentle touch
That heals my wounds
Your youthful smile
That turns my head
Your love rocket
That launches me into space
Where nothing else really mattered
But just your face, your beautiful self
40   Your beauty and your gentle touch
For your charming beauty
Haunt my youthful thoughts
For too long now
I have missed all these
For I have been starved
All these endless weeks
For I have eaten
Quite a little each day
And I have lost some weight
50   So it seems to me for I dream of you all night long
For I think of our days at the park
In the streets whose name is Love!
I dream of our days at sea
In the yacht whose name is *Santa Nma*
For I have a nostalgia
Of the great love we shared
In the home whose name is Lilies
For I long, I long
To see those your glittering eyes
60   Which calmed my nerves
After the hard day's work
I dream of those your graceful
Steps as you descend down
The staircase from above
Where our love abounds
In the real you

I have known of old
For I long for your warmth
Which has left me in the cold
70 For I do miss you here
Greater than ever before
For I was forced to seek
In the eyes of the alighting passengers
In the carbins of the standing airplane
Inside the empty seats
Of your supposed flight
In the eyes of the air hostesses
Right there on the lonesome lounge
I am searching and asking for you
80 From the manifest of your flight
My dear, I could not find your name
My heart is heavy and really in flames
My brain is cloudy and really confused
For many questions bother my troubled mind
For I am hoping all is well with you
For I have tried to gather my thoughts
To dial the key numbers to your heart
Expecting the usual warmth
That used to flow
90 From the warmth
And wind of your love
That blows our thoughts
But a cold silence greeted my ears
As I heard the reply
From the answering machine
While my heart yearned
For you on the line
In the prolonged expectation
Of your homecoming
100 For you did tell me
How much you really cared
How much you loved me
Why couldn't you come home?
As you did promise

And bring back home
The warmth of the house
For tomorrow is our wedding day.

12:00 noon
June 8, 1993
Abuja Airport
Gwagwalada

THE IMPORT OF YOUR SILENCE

The time is six-thirty in the morning
The Harmattan wind is blowing fierce
The weather is pretty cold and unfriendly
The much I can remember is that
I have myself wrapped up with my blanket
Coiled up like a helpless fetus
In the mother's womb waiting patiently
My sleep has been severally interrupted
With nightmares about your silence
10   My mind has been battling to solve
The mind bugging riddle of your silence
I remembered that there is a saying
Which goes like this!
"Silence is the best answer to a fool"
Then I asked myself how I have become a fool
For the sake of nothing but love
I may be a fool a thousand times
If you say so, but I will not give up
For come rain, come sunshine, my love remains
20   Then I ask myself, "Why does she accept my gifts?"
Could it be because mothers always say
"Accept whatever they may give you
Because you did not have to beg for it
For you make up your mind to love
Whom your heart is endeared to
For the riddle of love and affection
Is solved by ones heart at all times
For gifts are mere tokens
To express the feelings from one's heart

30	And the feelings many times are marginal
	For they do not have a defined focus
	For many of them are eager to be counted
	As one of the very few or very many
	Who have kissed your lips in flirtation
	In the endless experiments for an enduring romance
	For in the streets of love are thousands of men
	Many are out for the thirst of a date
	Without any iota of the true love
	For very few, indeed, very few love
40	Really from their hearts as should be
	And as such every girl should be
	On her guard to develop enough intuition
	To be in position of sieving the substance
	From the mountain of floating chaff
	For the game of love to a young girl
	Is the most difficult battle that every girl
	Passes through except a handful in the convent"
	For if I were a girl I will stand my ground
	I will build a wall made of rock
50	In my endless adventure in search of my true love
	For many have fallen into the hands of vampires
	For many have fallen into broken marriages
	For many have had nightmares of relationships
	Which ended in fiasco after great memories
	After sweet memories of a great honeymoon
	For relationships which never lasted to the end
	Leave enduring scars in some corners of our hearts
	For many times we make mistakes in our choice
	Not because we are fools per se
60	But because we fall in love with our hearts first
	Instead of our heads in the first instance
	For when we fall in love with our hearts
	At first, then our heads put the facts together
	To say this is not the true love
	And when we move in a direction for change
	Our hearts are shattered in some bits and pieces
	In the name of broken love . . . heartbreaks

We are mortals and with limited knowledge
But when we learn to fall in love first
70   With our heads, then we can assess
The terrain and features of our relationships
When the topography is too rough to be amended
Then we can tactically withdraw in style
And at the end we are happy without heartbreaks
However the truth remains that in all
You may call me a fool which indeed
I may actually have shown myself to be
But why have you continued to accept my gifts?
Why do you enjoy reading my long letters?
80   And you could never be moved to say
Just" thank you" for the little gifts
And to write and say "thank you"
For all my numerous cards and letters
Makes me accept the fool which you
Have indeed proved me to be
For despite every ugly treatment I got
I still stand my ground to plead
Even falling on my knees in my bedroom
And begging you to accept me
90   By merely calling your name—Nma
As I do not know when I could have the honor
The rare privilege, the greatest award
That could be bestowed on my mortal self
To live in the same house with you
To share my bed with you
To share my bathroom with you
To dine with you on my dining table
To plan things out with you
To share the baby's cries with you
100   To cook our food with you
To help wash our dishes with you
To shop in the market with you
To drive in the same car with you
To visit resort centers with you
To swim in the same pool with you

To open our lungs and laugh for fun
To quarrel with you and settle with you
For it is the true test of an enduring love
For the day I could sleep halfway at night
110   To feel your warmth on my side
Will be fully documented in my notebooks
For then my heart would have gotten
To an enduring climax of its desires
However, where the worst happens at last
Where the import of your long silence
Matures in the winds of time not as love
Then I want to promise the goddess of love
That till the end of my mortal existence
I will buy flowers and send to you
120   On all your birthdays all the days as you live
As a token of my unending love
For that may serve as an antidote
To preserve the energies in my mortal life
For I could not afford to blow off the candle flame
The enduring source of overwhelming inspiration
Which have gradually launched me into space
Filled with my unique fountain pen
And never finishing scribbling papers
For to forget you will be to forget my dreams
130   For I love the dreams that haunt my whole being
And you have come my way to make it come true
While I sit all night long and all day long
Scribbling away, doing one thing I love doing
For to stop loving you will leave me as
An unfulfilled ambitionless mortal floating across
As many have taken to live their lives
The import of your endless silence
May bring a lot of joy to my lovesick heart
It may also bring a lot of sadness to my heart
140   But no matter what happened at the end
My physical love may be nailed on a stake
But my spiritual love and the enduring inspiration
It has admiringly evoked in me lives on

It could never die
For I have fallen in love once in my life
For I have also had to accept that the love died
But my endless love for you could never die
For it could only die with me in the winds
For the love in my heart is real
150   For the love in my heart is pure
For the love in any heart is an innocent love
A love born from the spiritual world
An uncontaminated love without stain
For you could marry any man you choose
For you could love anyone you may wish
I know I could not be moved with jealousy
For my love for you have surpassed the physical
It has climbed many ladders to the white clouds
And ascended into the spiritual realm
160   Where we love not the flesh and blood
Like the mortal man was made with
But from the bloodless realm of existence
Frankly, I am really very tired and exhausted
In anticipation that one day you will bare your mind

9:55 am
January 7, 1994
Abuja Clinics Ltd
Karu, Abuja

"NOT HIM AGAIN"

For many boring and lonely minutes
For many endless times of counting seconds
For many countless spurring and racing hours
For many passing lonely and lonesome days
For many empty cold and lonely nights
For many fading memories of countless fortnights
For many crawling months which leave me in the limbo
For two good calendar years and more to count
I have borne the sickness of lovelorn all alone
10   My heart has filled without space for more
I could not any more carry the burden all alone
Then I thought it wise to share it with someone
It was my little niece, a late teenage girl
That I could trust to keep my secret to myself
For I never wanted anybody in my family to know
To know a single thing about Nma
For I wished to parcel her news as a bombshell
For they have wondered whether am human at all
For seldom do I bring girls home
20   For rarely could they associate me with any
But unknown to them is that my heart is somewhere
That Nma has stolen my heart in pretense
And taken it to the moon with my love shuttle
And then remained in the moon watching me
Roast every other day dying and crying for her
Asking her to bring my heart back to me
Or even to bring home my love shuttle
My romance spacecraft, so that if all fails
I could shuttle to the moon with some ease

30   To take my heart and keep it to myself
But Nma has said no, very bluntly
Refusing me, my heart, and hanging my love
At the crescent edge of the new moon
Watching my lovesick heart pine day and night
In a fruitless attempt to find my love
For Nma knows my heart in full
For Nma is my heart in frankness
For Nma is playing tricks with me
For she knows how much I can love
40   For she knows the magnitude of the love in me
For only her could tell the world
The power of affection passing through me
For only her could give me back my heart
For there could be only one reason
She has taken solace in stealing my heart
For she is fighting in pretense—
The exploding love she has for me
Building up in her day by day
Week by week moment by moment
50   For she finds it difficult to bare her mind
For she is scared I was going to take off
In a love spree and abandon her in emptiness
For she reads my heart all the time
In my endless long love letters
In my love-laden cards from the posts
Which open their doors to the entrance
With love songs which are soft to the heart
Which open the gate to the park whose name is Love
For the melody of the songs are sweet and tender
60   For the cards themselves sing like the love lark
For if the songs are played in the green Kubwa Hills
The inspiring hills themselves with their scenes
Would shake their waists and heads in tune
With the power of the lyrics and rhymes abound
For the queen of the virgins in the Kubwa Hills
Would be amused in the thrilling moment
That she may not know the exact time

She will hand over my Nma—my heart
To my lovesick self, searching every other day
70   Praying for a moment to behold the queen
The queen of love standing in the gate of my heart
For if the winds hear the tune of the music
Yes, the endearing tunes from those cards
They will dance a dance of love
In the great anticipation that at the end
My love will come back to me in one piece
For then the burden in my heart weighs me down
For then the grief of lovelorn pulls me apart
For then the loneliness of secret love
80   As I bared my mind to my little niece
Who promised to see Nma and talk with her
As intelligent and as bold and as womanly
As she proved to be, she undertook the voyage
Went to the peak of the Kubwa Hills as a virgin
Which indeed she is and saw my Nma
She engaged Nma in a long conversation
So as to read her mind and thought
Being a strange person to Nma
Nma was more curious and suspicious
90   And I did warn my niece to beware
They talked at length about school and gossiped
Then it was time to break the ice
To deliver the message of her love mission
Then she tactfully brought my sweet name
She mentioned my sweet name to Nma's hearing
Nma was mad at my name and lost her cool
To scream at my niece "No, not him again!"

1:30 pm
January 10, 1994
Abuja Clinics Ltd
Karu, Abuja

PLEASE DON'T SAY NO

It may seem your mind
Is so young and so tender
It may seem as succulent
As the sap of a virgin herb
Your thoughts may seem
As straight as a tree
Your emotions may be
As pathetic as a log of wood
And as indifferent as
10   A village Indian girl
For you may be as
Innocent as the leaves of grass
The truth remains
That you are human
As human and as fleshly
As an emotional mortal
For even a fetus
In the mother's womb loves
For even a day old
20   Feels and loves
How much more you
At nineteen your late teens
A woman enough
With enough room
To house Rome and Romulus
For all these troubles not withstanding
One thing I do know
From deep inside me
Is that I am head over heels

30   In love with you
For the love in my eyes
Sees nobody else
It yearns of no one else
For the love in my heart
Yearns for no one
Not any girl
Not any young woman
But your supple blues
For I seem confused
40   For I do not know
What to do with myself
For the elegance of your beauty
And the wit and brilliance
In your brains
Have swept me away
In their great currents
Blindfolding me
In your captive aura
Trapping my emotions
50   Leading me blindly into your waves
Enveloping my emotions in its mist
Trapping me as a love fish
In your sweeping net
Struggling passionately
For your helping hand
For you have drifted
My thoughts into isolation
For I am as helpless
As a day-old chick
60   Abandoned in the open
To the mercy of the hawks
For I do not know
Where to go
For your beauty
And your composite self
Is a bait in the fishing hook
Which has trapped me

In a helpless mood
For you have imprisoned my feelings
70   For you have encapsulated my thoughts
Spurring my spirit into soaring heights
For I could not love without you
For my heart is empty
For my mind is lonesome
Without the warmth
And the fire inside you
For I am in a wreck
Drowning in your love
For I cannot love
80   Not again without you
For the game of love
Has been unfair to me
For.my heart has been hurt
A great deal in the past
For my heart has been hurt
Lost in the limbo
For I am lost in the angry sea
Without your compass thumb
For I am living in the limbo
90   Please don't let me drown
Lend me a helping hand
And put together
The bits and pieces
Left of my lovesick heart
While I plead to the softest spots
Of your feminine intoxicating heart
As I plead on and on
"Please don't say no"
And drown a lovesick heart
100   In the frostbite of snow.

2:40 pm
July 11, 1993
Kubwa, Abuja

Don't You Know

Today I found myself
Sitting on a brown log of wood
In a lonesome grassland
Where only the buzz of the bees
The chirp of the grasshoppers
The songs of birds
The drone of a distant airplane
The noise of the passing car
The croaking of a frog
10   The whistling of the passing wind
The happiness of the leaves of grass
Remind me of my love
For of late, you have been silent
You have not cared to write
You have not even remembered me
My dear, I wish to ask you
One simple question
That has given me sleepless nights
That has given me nightmares
20   And that is my dear
Don't you know?
How much you mean to me?
Don't you know?
The influence you wield in my life?
Don't you know?
That my life is sad without you?
Don't you know?
That you are hurting me?
My dear, don't you know?

30   That I am lost without you?
That my life is empty
That I have nobody
Just nobody to talk to
Nobody to go out with
Nobody to love
Nobody to read my poems to
Don't you know?
That you are everything
Yes, everything good
40   That happened to my life
Don't you know?
How much I have missed you
Don't you know?
I am lonely here
In this desert grass plains
Where the songs of birds
Remind me of everything about you
Where the passing winds
Even whistle your name across
50   Where the humming birds
Hum your usual tunes
Where the day is dull
Without your usual humor
Where the ripples in the brook
Re-echo a desolate tune
Where even the clouds
In the distant sky
Squeeze their face in isolation
Where the melodious songs of birds
60   Have lost their magic touch
Where the beauty of nature
Makes very little meaning
Where I seek for a muse
To keep my idle pen busy
But none comes my way
Where the eclipse of the sun
Throws the earth into the dark

Where the distant green hills
Have lost their romance
70   With the dazzling blue sky
Where the rain never falls
Where pretty women
Have lost their gift of God
Where the glamour of youth
Never shines anymore
Where the fire of love
Has died down in frustration
Where the beauty of the rose
Have lost its natural powers
80   Where the glitter of gold
Never sees the light of the day
For the sun remains behind
Hiding and weeping
Behind the clouds
Where the air is very still
Where no wind blows across
To brighten the day
Where the moon never beams
Don't you know, my dear?
90   That my life here
Is like Crusoe's
For I am lost in the wilderness
Just only me without you
Don't you know my dear?
That your gentle touch
Makes the leaves of grass
To smile to a bright day
That your prolonged absence
Has reduced me into a hermit
100   Don't you know?
How much I missed
Our long evening walks
In the garden parks
Where the rose buds
Caress our caring minds

Where the evening winds
Kiss the falling leaves
Making a crumbling rustling noise
Like a gentle crispy crunch
110   When you hold my hands
While we explore our minds
Even asking the wind
Which way to blow your hair?
Dropping down your shoulder blades
Like that of a sea goddess
Don't you know?
That you are my pearl
The apple of my eyes
The honey in my tea
120   My precious pot of gold
Don't you know my dear?
That your heartbeat
Yes, the *lub dub* of your heart
Tells me how much you cared
Don't you know?
That you have left me
Too long a time
In the cold of the green Kubwa Hills
Don't you know?
130   That it is very lonely here
Can't you see my dear?
That my life has changed
That my happiness
Has gone with the winds
That my light of the day
Has melted in the sun
That the moonlighting
Has made me sick
For I have no one
140   To take a walk with me
That your undue absence
Has done much harm
To my love sick heart

Can't you see?
That you mean too much to me
Don't you know?
That I am in love
Like I have never been before
That I am in love
150   Not with the flowing sea
Not with the rainbow spree
Not with the water falls
Not with the golden walls
Not with the laughing dove
Not with the pen-pal love
Not with the songs of birds
Not with the passing winds
Not with the leaves of grass
Not with ripples of the brook
160   Not with the setting sun
Not with the moon lighting
Not with the distant green hills
Not with the white clouds
Not with the verses you evoke
But with the person in you
The love you unfolded in me
Driving me into the mountain clouds

5:00 pm
July 25, 1993
Kubwa Hills
Abuja

Bond Of Love

The day is a quiet one
The sun is setting
Down the distant green hills
Where the clouds and the hills
Hold hands in endless romance
Cheating on the blue sky
Which makes their bed
As rosy and as romantic
As a quiet cool evening
10   Where I am sitting
On an anthill
And looking up into the hills
The beauty of the green Kubwa Hills
Which has married the muse
That clouds my youthful brain
On a crucible where love reigns
Where love is supreme
Where love is enthroned
In naked loneliness
20   Where the muse of love
Plays on and on and on
Now it is half past five
The setting sun is grazing
Across my lovesick mind
Lighting a candle of love
For my evening date
In frantic wholesome desire
For your hand in the aisle
For then I dream great dreams

30   When we will own the world
When we will explore the hills
When we will go for a swim
When we will hold each other's arm
When we will snore away
In a world for only two of us
In a world just for you and me
In a world where I sing songs
For only your lucky ears
In a world where your laughter endures
40   In a world we will conquer
Just the two of us
Passing through the roaring waves
Passing through the burning flames
Passing through the babies' cries
Passing through the breakfast table
Passing through a time of sadness
Passing through a time of joy
In a world where nothing really matters
Except the two of us
50   In a world where I will
Cook some food for you
In a world where
You will make my bed
In a world where our flowers will grow
Inch by inch as we water them
Day by day, lending each other a hand
Here on the anthill
We will build our home
We will paint it pink
60   Or ash as you may wish
And we will hang your picture frame
Smiling on our walls
Holding my hand in need
With your white gown
Flowing down your toes
And stretching far behind
Like a peacock show

In a royal bridal train
Where the joy of laughter
70   The clapping of hands
The drinking of wine
In sealed happiness
Follow our days home
As you may sob in your mum's arms
As she consoles you deeply
Admonishing you then
That this is your chance
Which you must seize
For you it may be a world
80   An entirely new world
Where you may be found wanting
Where you may be found deficient
Where you may be found groping
Groping in the darkness of love
For you need not to bother
For I am there to lend you
A helping hand
A hand of love in need
A love in bond
90   The beauty of a bond
The bond of love
After which our life
Will then start for us
We will be free as the winds
To explore the world
With the aura and delight
Of our youthful reach
For a time comes
When two people make up their minds
100   To sail to sea on a voyage
A voyage full of ups
A voyage full of downs
A voyage full of ups and downs
At the mercy of the sea
At the mercy of the waves

Tossing us here and there
Pushing us in and out
Throwing us to and fro
Making us gloom and bright
110   Giving us pains and laughter
Lacing our day with joy
Visiting us in times of want
Brightening us in times of plenty
Comforting us in times of sorrow
For our life we got to live
Just the two of us
My dear, I may be boring you
For just a sentence
I am keen to express
120   In these great lines
Which may be rosy
Which may be confusing as well
I wish to ask you my dear
Will you marry me?
Come home with me
Where you are the queen
And I am the king
In an empire we will build
To endure the test of the times
130   With the helping hand of God.

6:15 pm
July 25, 2993
Kubwa, Abuja

ENDLESS LOVE

I have written ten letters now
I have mailed ten postcards then
All in all none has steered
Your youthful but love-proof heart
I have been to the foot and peak
East of the panoramic green Kubwa Hills
I have asked the kites and the winds
About you, your beautiful self
They reassured me that you are fine
10   As fine as the morning rain
For all this long while
You have played the princess
Which indeed you are
The elegant princess of Eluama
You have made up your mind
And abandoned me in the colds
And in the endless rains of love
Falling cats and dogs in fright
Here east of Kubwa green hills
20   Where men are never born
You have left me to die
With an empty and lovesick heart
You have not heard my pleas
You have not heard my messages
Brought to you by the kites and the winds
You could not lend me a hand
You could not lend me a helping hand
To arise and shine from my bed

For I am sick in a love bed
30   Dreaming and dreaming of you
Praying and imploring the goddess
Of love to rescue me from the grips
From the endless wine of love
For the leaves of grass are crying
Though they were once very happy
Asking me every other day
About my princess on a long trip
For I promised them you will be home
For then the leaves of grass were singing
40   They were singing love songs
For then the clouds were happy
For then the rocks were waiting
Endlessly for your majestic return
But your silence has left us in the limbo
And the rocks are cracking in frustration
The green Kubwa Hills have lost their charm
The green of the green Kubwa Hills are fading
For the leaves of grass are weeping
For the clouds have refused to descend
50   To commune with the virgins at the peak
East of the panoramic green Kubwa Hills
For my mind and thoughts
Have been on sentry
At the outpost whose gate
Has love boldly written on it
For now I am tired
For now I have grown weary
For all the youthful energies
Has gone asleep in neglect
60   For the man in me has slept
For though my morale is low
From the weary songs of love
For my throat has gone dry
In all my attempts to win your heart
For I have exhausted the arrows

In my once heavy love sick quiver
Shooting endlessly into the sky
Caressing only the winds of love
Without a moment to kiss my Petals of Rose
70 For fear of the next method
Which you will apply to turn me down
For I am bored and tired
In anticipation that my lines
Could steer your youthful virgin heart
To board my little ship *Santa-Venus*
For my endless love are still dreams
For I am not ashamed indeed
Of having written all I have
All the unending love letters
80 Which could wake the dead
From their still and silent graves
Which could steer even Lady Macbeth
To spare the brains of the innocent child
But they have not steered the hair
Yes, the single hair on your head
For I never know that princesses
Could be as cold as you—
Have indeed proved to be
For the cold winds from you
90 Have blown off the fire in me
And I have lost the nerves
To love again like of old
For all I have done to love
As seen in the petals of rose
I do not have any regrets
For at the end of the day
I have accepted the big fool
Which you have made of me
Just for the name of love
100 Despite all said and undone
My love for you never dies
For even when I live and die

It lives on and on the more
For it cannot die with me
For it lives on forever
In the peak of the green Kubwa Hills
Where the blood in the veins
Of petals of rose flows on and unendingly
Though my spirit has gone damp
110   For my rivals have been right
For they laughed at me in scorn
For loving a girl—the wind
While the wind is in love with the rain
For then I did fight back
To defend your youthful heart
Hoping that one day my love
Will remember me and come home
But my rivals have proved me wrong
And I have fallen into bits and pieces
120   In the pedestal of unreserved love
For though my hands are tied
In my unending love for you
For I cannot stop loving my girl
For you are my girl, my endless inspiration
For you are mine, just for me
In our creative world of romance
Where angels serve as muse
That ruffles our minds, our kinds
In the blinds of the love we create
130   Within the four walls of our psyche
For now I'd accept in full
That the game of love
Has been unfair to me
For I have basked in the lakes
Of love, be it warm or cold
For I have dreamt dreams
Where love grows on trees
Where love sings like wren
Where love passes like the winds

140   Where love cares like a mother
        Where love flies freely like the birds
        Where love makes honey like the bees
        Where love blossoms like queen of the night
        Where love beams like the moon
        Where love rises like the sun
        Where love sets before it is dawn
        Where love chirps like a swallow
        Where love kisses the clouds
        When the dawn shakes hands
150   With the fading twilight
        For I have pleaded for love
        For I have cried for love
        For I have never been loved
        For though my lovesick heart
        Yearns forever for you
        For I do not envy the Jones
        Who have the key to your heart
        Those kings and princes
        Whom your heart is after
160   Whom your heart yearns for
        For you may learn to love
        For any man born of a woman
        Could pretend to love you
        But none could give you
        Any love close to what my heart
        Has indeed offered to give
        For my heart has sworn
        To the clouds of the green Kubwa Hills
        That I will keep loving you
170   Till the last days of my mortal life
        Though you may have neglected me
        Abandoning me to the hands and care
        Of the innocent winds of time
        Which has promised something new
        Today and every other day
        Pleading with me to reach out

In blindfold and love
Some body real, and not anymore
Through the none replied messages
180   Carried by the wings of the winds
Through an endless love of the blinds

5:45 pm
October 2, 1993
Kubwa, Abuja

LOST IN KUBWA HILLS

Here I am still seeking
Here I am still single
Here I am still empty
Here I am still scouting
Here I am still combing
Here I am still searching
For you in the hills
I am looking for you
Here in the green Kubwa Hills
10   Where the day is kind
The leaves are forest green
The rocks are romantic
Their color is brown here
Their color is grey there
The birds are singing
On the treetops
Just above my head
The wind is kissing my lips
My dry and cracking lips
20   Which you have long left
And abandoned to the mercies
Of the Harmattan winds
Here on top of green Kubwa Hills
Where the weather is kind
To my roughened skin
Which has gone coarse
In the believe and frankness
That I may still find
My love here in the hills

30   For I am chatting
With the leaves of grass
With the bark of the trees
With the withering rocks
With the lonely lost bees
With the innocent butterflies
Who perch on my palm
In a bid to lend a hand
To my lonesome and craving heart
Lost in the woods
40   Lost in the rocks
Lost in the plains
Lost in the brooks
Lost in the streams
Lost in the lonely roads
In the empty rooms
In the cold beds
Where the thoughts of you
Have stolen my light of day
Where my preoccupation
50   About our broken love
Have haunted my broken heart
For it may seem to be bad
For our time may seem to end
For our love may have hit the rocks
Just like I am talking
To the silent rocks
Which apparently had no hands
In the disaster that has befallen
Our long cherished love
60   For I know that we are humans
For I know that I have erred
Saying that I have wronged you
Is just re-echoing the obvious
For I do not believe
That our love will end
Here in the rocks
Here in the cold green Kubwa Hills

Where I have taken solace
With the songs of birds
70   The whispering of the springs
The hissing of the rattle snakes
The whistling of the passing wind
The noisy exhaust of distant cars
The rumbling noise of the brooks
For I wish to appeal to you
That we may resolve
To turn a new leaf
For the faults may be mine
For the faults may be yours
80   For now that may not matter
The wrongs have been made
For our hearts have been bruised
For that may be just enough
To rekindle the love
The great love we shared
The love that has been with us
Since the past years
The love that glows
In our hearts of old
90   Please, dear, let's turn a new leaf
Let's forget the past
For we are born humans
For we are born imperfect
For we have our faults
For we have our good parts too
For in you is a great woman
A lady I have come to respect
The only woman that has the key
The real key to my heart
100   For I may pretend
That all is well with me
The truth remains
That my life is lonely
That my life is lifeless
That there is no joy

Here, in my broken heart
That my life is meaningless
That my being is sad
That my emotions are sorrowful
110   Without your gentle self
As I have known no peace
Since these months we parted
For I have looked for happiness
I have sought for affection
I have searched for joy
I have pleaded for goodness
I have longed for a thrill
I have tried to attract love
With my hard earned money
120   All has been in the wind
All has not been the same
All has not been as before
All has lost the usual touch
All has been eroded away
All I seem to do at will
Never paid off as it should
Please I am indeed sorry
I may have been too hard
On your gentle and tender heart
130   I may have hurt your inner self
I may have wronged you greatly
Please do not let all that
Bother your youthful heart
For my love is only in you
For only you understand the man
The real person in me
For only you has been patient
To put the many parts
That makes up my composite self
140   Into their rightful places
My dear, I am sorry
For the mistakes of the past
For the wrongs done

To our hearts from my side
And from your side
For too many wrongs
May never make a right
But the accumulation of wrongs
Could form a reconciliation platform
150   To consider the righting
Of our numerous wrongs
And a new accord
A new platform of compromise
Could be reached in sincere attempts
To make good the wrongs
For nothing in life
Ever reaches a near perfection
Without the hand of errors
For from the blunders
160   Of our past life
We can reshape our future
Just for the sake of our hearts
For the sake of this love
The great love we shared
For the love we shared
In the days that have gone
Not really with the wind
But the days that have gone
With the aim to lend a hand
170   A mending hand
To put ourselves together
And start building for the future
For from the wrongs and rights
Of our innocent and wholesome past
We can make peace
For a more peaceful tomorrow
For then we have a baseline
To fall back upon in the future
When next trouble strikes
180   Please, my dear, my love
Don't let me die

Don't harden your heart
As there is still a future
A good future for us to amend
A future to cherish as ours
A future to smile in your arms
A future to keep and protect
A future for you and me
A future for our family to come
190   A future to endure
And rear our kids
And watch them grow
On a healthy platform
Of our irrevocable reconciliation
For you could in the process
Save my dying youthful heart
From utter ruin
Which may seem imminent
For I am lost here
200   In the thicket of the green Kubwa Hills
Lost in the panoramic green Kubwa Hills
Here where the day
Has been laced with little joy
Where the weather is kind
To my shaken and troubled heart
Where the leaves of grass
Are asking me about you
Where the butterflies are itching
To see your pretty face
210   To see you again
Where the hills
Have noticed your long absence
Where the radiance of your beauty
Has only left dullness behind
Where your justly troubled heart
Aches even in my mind's eye
Pricking my helpless heart
In the agony of the love
In the agony of the pain

220   In the agony of the love and pain
        In the agony of attempts
        To muster enough courage
        Throwing my usual ego
        Into the winds
        Because I am convinced
        That I still love you dearly
        For I am bored living alone
        For I am tired searching for you
        In the empty spaces
230   In the empty hills
        In the empty rocks
        In the open spaces
        In the troubled dreams
        As I pray you to come home
        And rescue me from here
        In this lonesome green Kubwa Hills

5:00 pm
July 22, 1993
Kubwa, Abuja

Winds of Love in Hard Times

Dear Peggy,
It is now four months
Since we last parted
I have had to bear
The loneliness which haunt
My lonely and youthful heart
For I try to comfort myself
But it is no use trying
For my heart is heavy
10   For my heart is worried
To say I am missing you
Will amount to trivializing
The emptiness in me
For of late it has not been
Quite rosy with me
Though I have been able
To get a job at hand
Which I will manage meanwhile
But my heart is not there
20   For life has been sour
A bit hard on me
For I have resorted to
Squatting with a friend
Who has been too nice
To feed me when he can
For, dear, the times are hard
Somehow I feel sorry
For my friend for the troubles
I am making him to pass through

30   Though he does not complain
        He is bearing it with a good heart
        He even gives me pocket money
        To enable me to keep going
        Till when I have worked
        To be paid a wage
        To minimize his burden
        I share his bed with him
        I share his plates with him
        I share his wardrobe with him
40   He is quite a friend at heart
        All that notwithstanding dear
        My days are hard here
        My heart seems really lost
        My whole life seems meaningless
        My whole plans seem hopeless
        For the problems in the country
        Have thrown my plans
        Into the passing wind
        I have written my GRE as proposed
50   The exams were pretty tough
        The worst thing that is making me crazy
        Is that my proposed university
        In New York City
        Has denied me admission
        For reasons not quite clear
        Apart from immigration issues
        To my troubled mind
        I have known little peace
        My ambition seems
        To be running down slowly
60   For of late, I have had nightmares
        That the embassy refused
        To give me visa to travel
        I know there is no place like home
        But here is no more like home
        For there is no peace here
        For there is no room for comfort here

No room to plot my usual graphs
About what could happen in the future
Life now seems meaningless
70 For here I am having it really rough
I had earlier planned
That even if I don't travel abroad
In pursuit of my doctorate
I could get a job
A good-paying job
Even then I have lost patience
With the trend of things
In this our country
Could you believe it?
80 I eat just once a day
When my friend could afford it
Most of the time
I have to buy
A small packet of five cookies
And a bottle of Coca Cola
Merely to appease my gastric juice
To pacify my gastric enzymes
Keeping away from developing—
A possible gastric or duodenal ulcer
90 So for now I lived on junk food
I go to work on empty stomach
And I eat just a donut
With a bottle of soda
That is my meal for the day
Funny enough I am
A university graduate
A first-class material
From the country's premier university
But I am languishing in the woods
100 Chasing blind and meaningless shadows
Though the days are hard for me
I wish to reassure you
That my love for you
Still burns really high

For I do miss you greatly here
For I do not even have the means
To come down to see you
For I do hope that
You do not mistake my troubles
110   With my love and affection for you
For I woke up quite early to write
In the twilight of the morning
The whole place here is quiet
The dew drops on the leaves
Of some ornamental plants
In the front of this house
Are dropping down gently
Like the innocent lovesick tears
Falling down on my pages
120   Where I poured my heart down
I am so emotionally down
That I am even shedding tears
Though I do not know why
Maybe because I do miss you greatly
Maybe for my love for you
Maybe I love you very much
Maybe not, maybe am hungry
Maybe life is too hard on me
Maybe I have missed you
130   For too long a time now
Last night I had a troubled sleep
Our time together haunted me
I could not sleep well
I rolled around the bed
All night long
Finding my poor self
Even screaming out 'Peggy!'
In my sleep, waking my friend up
Who then asked what the problem is
140   As I replied, "It is just a nightmare"
For in my dream you paid a visit
I took my time to explain things out

But you were very unhappy
You were not sympathetic
I tried to explain myself
But you would not listen
You left my friend's house
Walking away in disgust
I pleaded for you to understand
150 It was all in vain
Like acts in dreams
You waved down a young man
Cruising across in his Lexus
And jumped in to your comfort
I could not stand it
I thought it was in real life
As such I screamed out
I yelled your name
That my nightmarish scream
160 Was overhead in our real world
I could not stand the shame
I asked myself 'what is this?
What is this all about?'
I had no answers
A thick smoke clouded my head
Then later it reached my eyes
I felt tears coming down my eyes
Dropping down like the dew drops
Falling down from the leaves
170 In sympathy to my tears
To my painful sobs
Peggy dear, I am so confused
I am so lonely, so poor
So disorganized, so helpless
So troubled, so emaciated
That not withstanding however
I know I am young
Not just young, I am strong
I also have the brains
180 To apply myself to use

Maybe not to immediate
Financial-yielding benefits
For I have been writing a lot
Quite a lot of late
For I do hope
That maybe a publisher
May equally appreciate my work
And in the attempt publish them
Maybe some royalty
190   May accrue at last
To provide some relief
To this poverty state
For now I still have enough resources
To buy myself some ink pens
And some papers
Which is keeping me
Pretty busy in writing
Pouring out inspirations
From my innermost being
Pouring down my heart
220   In the attitude and manner
Of something I loving doing most
Writing
I know I have a father
I know I have a mother
I know I have two brothers
I know I have two sisters
They have all played their cards well
They have all done their best
From childhood they have nursed
230   They have clothed, they have trained
They have loved me greatly
I feel really ashamed to go home
Looking like a prodigal son
Which you know too well am not
I have got to chart my course
I have got to build my future
I have got to save for myself

Keeping some behind
To keep our souls alive
240   During the rainy day
Dear Peggy, my aim
Is to reassure you
That my love for you
Will never die
For if ever it will
It will die with me
I do not know
How you view things now
I do not know your decisions
250   I am lost about your ambitions
I am troubled about your plans
Could it be that you
Don't care anymore?
Could it be you are bored of writing?
Could it be you have found
A new love to cherish?
I do not know
But I don't want to believe
That anything can come between us
260   Though, I do recognize
That the twin efforts
Of distance and time
Could tarnish the luster of love
They could burn out the candle flame
To the tail and peril of diminishing returns
And if not rekindled again
Drops out into the dark
Letting in the devils hand
To break a bond of love
270   Which was made in sincerity
Which was made in good faith
Peggy, when you find time
Please do keep me in the know
For my life is moody
Without your gentle self

Adding some humor
Lacing my days with love
Extend a benevolent hand of love
At this very time I need it most
280   Peggy, here I am sitting alone
On my friend's drawing stool
Writing on his drawing board
For he is an architect
Looking outside through the louvers
I could see some flower hedges
Some of the leaves are green
Some are yellow, some are maroon
Some are red, some are neither red
Nor scarlet, some are variegated
290   Like the water lilies of Adaoma Lake
Around them are grey-colored gravels
Which added some beauty
To their happiness and life
Around the table are papers
Drawing papers, tracing papers
T-square, graduated rule, drawing pens
A bunch of keys, a broken mirror
Some magazines and old newspapers
My Everite wrist-watch trotting away
300   The room is small as expected
On my left is a wooden bed
On my right is a chair
On my right is also a window
From where I see and admire
The brilliant light of the day
My only source of joy
The room is a bit scattered
It may need to be tidied up
I seem not to be in the mood
310   My friend has just left for work
I am on call this afternoon
As such I had to write
Good-bye, my love

My faithful princess
I am hoping that the benevolent
Winds of love
Will lend us a helping hand
Your endless love,

7:00 am
July 22, 1993
Kubwa, Abuja

CRESCENT GREEN KUBWA HILLS

Standing endlessly at a T-junction lost in thought
Waiting patiently for a bus to go in search of the love of my life
I looked up and beheld the glory of God's unique creation
Of the scenic beauty and the unforgettable memories
Of the romantic green Kubwa landscape
Undulating gently down in unique panoramic beauty
To the foot of the rolling soft green peaks
Running into an enclosure like a marine cove
Forming a half moon with the splendor of evergreen
10   Stretching from my extreme right to the east
Into a dome of a dish like the DC capitol
Enveloping the inhabitants with their daily busy lives
Fortifying the settlers in the green Kubwa Hills
Spreading out its wings in protective embrace
Like a mother hen does with her motherly instincts
To protect her young to perpetuate her unique progeny
When the hawk swoops and hollers in desperation
Hunting for a meal to feed her young and keep the race
In this drifting love boat where I hopefully ride
20   I found myself dreaming of great things to come
Drifting away into endless possibilities that life could offer
In this romance with the green Kubwa Hills
While I imagined what love holds for us beyond
At the peak of the enigmatic topographic beauty
What color of lark to behold in its magnificence?
Singing its endless songs of love with a compelling passion
To the ears of the silent hills in great admiration
Sometimes even to the lapping gentle streams
Tongues of the ripples in an endless dance of love

30   Leaping across little rocks romancing the pebbles
        From the meandering rivulet as it makes its way
        Finding their paths to this haunting love saga
        Amongst the rugged vests of an enchanting love
        Of these magnificent rocks patiently enduring our metaphors
        Adoring the unique satellite haven of lasting inspiration
        Stretching South Westwards
        From the shaking Aso Rock
        The seat of trembling power west of the Niger
        Of one giant in the equatorial tropics of mother Africa
40   Towering emptily to the clouds
        Lacking the wisdom of the ancients
        Which endured in the vicinity
        Not too long ago along the banks of the great Nile
        Giving a human face in democratic attributes
        To the tourist Zuma Rock in our midst
        Reminding one of the gateways to a lasting political freedom
        Into the territory of Abuja the seat of the future of Africa
        About questions without answers in poor governance
        On what really goes on in our government in Aso Hills
50   Behind those rocky busy hills overlooking
        That crescent inspiring gorgeous green Kubwa Hills
        Where an endless love in great anticipation for tomorrow
        Lavishly heaped on landscape in the little town of Kubwa
        Reminds a young man lost in the incandescent fire of youth
        About an unduly delayed long expectant illusive date
        He is too eager to experience for once in his mortal life.

        8:50 am
        September 16, 1993
        FHA T-junction
        Kubwa, Abuja

Behind The Crescent Kubwa Hills

On a lonely walk
Going up a gentle hill
In the neighborhood
Of Gwagwalada Crescent
I remembered my love
In the twilight of the evening
A young man and his girl
Walked slowly across
Murmuring some sweet nothings
10   Into each other's ears
Then I remembered my love
The love I have longed for
The girl in the center
Of my youthful heart
The girl whose letter
Sends an upsurge of adrenaline
Down into my blood stream
Signaling to my lovesick heart
As it beats and pounds
20   Much harder than ever
Before hurrying into its contents
With great expectations
To see may be something
To console my lonely heart
From the grips of lonesomeness
Which makes my quiet moments

A time of reflection
A time of quietude
A time of supplication
30   A time of soliloquy
Pleading with the silent hills
Pleading with the inspiring hills
To please tell the eagles
Who visit her hill tops
That they should fly
Fast to the east
To tell my love
That my life here
Is sad and unfulfilled
40   That my heart is empty
And out of touch
With the reality of our times
That my feelings
That my emotions
Has climbed to the peak
Of the crescent green Kubwa Hills
Searching endlessly for her
Calling her name
Pleading with the winds
50   Pleading with the winds of love
To reach her inner hearts
And tell her my mind
That my mind is blue
That my mind is snow site
That my mind is green
Like the innocent leaves of grass
That my thoughts are petals of rose
That my evening is empty
That my whole self is lost
60   On the other side of love
Where there is nothing more
But just the fire of love

Burning endless in a strong flame
Maybe unknown to my heart
Behind the crescent green Kubwa Hills

7:40 pm
September 17, 1993
Kubwa, Abuja

A Night Before

"Hello!
Good morning
Please may I speak to Nma?
Hello, princess Nma
It is me, my dear
Your heartthrob
How are you doing?
I am sorry waking you up
So early this morning
10   Just to hear your silver voice
From the telephone earpiece
Just to let you know
How much you mean to me
Hope you enjoyed your sleep
Did you enjoy your sleep?
Were you sleeping in my arms?
Tell me what was your dream?
I hope no wonder guy
Stole your heart in your dream
20   While my ghost stood there
Sulking like acts in dreams
Here I am as fine as rain
The day is quite bright
The clouds are white
Like little puppies
The sky is clean like Maclean
Here in my home
My country home
Overlooking the sea

30   Looking down the window
To the empty sea
I could see two yachts
Through the lens of my binoculars
Approaching from the south end
Some two hundred nautical miles
Northeast to my home
Two flying boats
Have just cruised pass
The roaring angry sea
Actually woke me up
40   Telling me it is a new day
The mist is gathering
In the earlier clear sky
Though the day still looks bright
The sun is only peeping out
From the far Eastside
As if it is afraid
To show up well
And shower us
With his effectual rays of warmth
50   His rays of blessing
His blessing of love
That visits our hearts
Day after day without pay
Yet, it is always faithful
The lucky old sun
Must be in love
With us little mortals
Who enjoy his warmth
Which adds more fun
60   To our daily endeavors
While we toil day after day
Even without remembering the sun
The lucky old sun
There in the Far East
Where the sun is peeping out
From the ocean of a blue sea

The scene is glorious
It is indeed an orange world
Splashing endlessly in a liquid mirror
70   Bathing the magnificence
Of the rainbow blue sea
Spreading out its numerous
Broom sticks like splendid
Hand of the living God
Showering his infinite
Blessings to our mortal hearts
Who have lost his maiden favors
In the great paradise lost
And now making a turn
80   For the better options
Of regaining the paradise
Where there will be no pain
No suffering, no sadness and no death
From the eye of a bard
I could visualize that paradise
From the imports and glory
Of this rising sun
For it must have been
The true scene of the lost paradise
90   Where God once came down
To commune with little mortals
And even little mortals
Were freely talking with him
It must have been
A glorious time"
"Hello! My dear
Are you still there?
Am very sorry I got carried away
Really am very happy
100   I am not boring you after all
And that in fact you feel
Very, very special
Listening to my voice
Rattling away this early morning

Do you remember your last visit?
It was from the direction
Of my descriptions
That the moon beamed
Showering us with
110   Her ineffectual rays
When we went to sea
Our moments in my boat
Our days in my new flying boat
Where we did bath
In the moon light orange glow
Cruising in the quiet sea
While you caressed
The passing waves
Watching the full moon
120   Bathing us in her beams
Reaching just the two of us
In a world where our love
Means more than the world
Yes where our love means
More than this ephemeral world
For we could afford
To hand the world over
To the care of the moon
While we have our cruise
130   In the moon lighting
Listening to the lapping waves
Of the talking sea
Whispering her sweet nothing
To the ears of her lover
In her endless romance
With the emperor of the sea
Humming like the birds
Crying like the winds
Hooting like the owl
140   Chatting like the weaver birds
Grumbling like the thunder
Glittering like the lighting

From the seat of God's throne
In the holy heavens
From where he showers us
With his infinite blessings
Blessings just for the two of us
Just the two of us
In our little world
150 Where we float in arms
In the love orange sea
For I wish to tell you
My dear that my sabbatical leave
Starts in exactly seven days
I will like you to accompany me
To the island of the Bahamas
Where I will write a new book
Where I will tell the world
How much you mean to me
160 In a manner they will understand
Will you make the trip with me?
Then get your things ready
We are taking off next weekend
You will be with me
In the Bahamas
The Island of the Coconut Sea
You will come over here
To join me and pack our luggage
A night before
170 See you then
Good-bye my love".

6:00 pm
July 25, 1993
Phase II site I
Kubwa, Abuja

TRIALS OF PRINCESS DIANA

Battered in the triangle of Highgrove bears
The royal dove cooed in endless tears
Hovered from one royal branch to another
Timelessly searching for a comforting love chamber
All her spirited trials met Buckingham deafness
The innocent love lark lived in lonesomeness
There was no hairy warm chest to curdle
There were no sweet memories to peddle
Diana was alone with haunting nightmares
10   While Highgrove smiles into emptiness
She lived a princess without spirited ale
She is a mother—a sympathetic nightingale
She loves from the innocence of her sincerity
She craves love she missed in childhood
She is denied love again in adulthood
But Diana is a mortal in flesh
But Diana is not a goldfish
Which jumps into trough of royal dives
In amusement to loved British wives
20   Diana is human as good as any woman
Desired to be loved by a man
But she was lonely with London cold
Without any love at all to uphold
And in faraway continent of Africa
I sat with her biography missing America
Then innocent feeling of pity clouded me
I could not drink my morning tea
My empty heart was heavy for Diana

I journeyed not with sweet love banana
30   But with emptiness of my love for Nma
The legendary virgin princess of Eluama
On that lonely road I walked alone
On that empty street love was gone
And my heart yelled out without echo
Laboring in cold silence of wall gecko
I saw the innocent Diana in emptiness
Languishing between those beautiful snapshots of happiness
Lies one of the most neglected princesses
Europe has produced in this century's excesses
40   Far above the gloom of hidden sadness
Smiling now and then with all readiness
Lives one of the most neglected ladies
Britain has ever chronicled in Buckingham diaries
For Diana is a snowdrop of beauty
For Diana is an apple dewdrop of artistry
For Diana is a love song beauty sings
Even back then in the serene Althorps
Where love larks sing on tree tops
While the wind whistles across the leaves
50   Children played hide and seek between trees
They hunted for eggs in pigeon nests
And perceived the aroma the kitchen zests
They learnt to gallop on a horseback
They tended to their pets with a bark
Only back then did Diana really love
For her innocence rejects nightmarish Highgrove
Shielding her from the woes of marriage
Packaging her whole into an empty carriage
Galloping down the horrors of fairy tales
60   Wallowing in ocean depths of angry whales
Dropping her into a utopian love island
Where royal beads grow as love diamonds
And there are no dimples for decorations
And empty mortals languish in untold isolation
Burying their feelings inside vaults of celebrities

Dying slowly in a world of niceties
Crying day and night in loveless matrimony
While the fox of Highgrove steals her honey
Leaving her empty in her own territory
70   While Britons watch this melodrama battery
In rapt silence while the princess of Wales
Stumbled from the peak to her tails
Crying for help from Highgrove to Kensington Palace
Pleading to be rescued from Buckingham's disgrace
Somehow the worst may have happened
But Diana is not to be blamed
For she was living in an empty wedlock
Performed by the imperial gods to mock
And toy with ease in reckless immunity
80   As we watch with remorse and pity
Seemingly the only role indeed to play
As we helpless mortals have no say
The gods hire and fire with ease
The gods never err as to sneeze
But the mortals daily pine under yokes
We have no hand in its strokes
For many a time I have wondered
Why Eves have been cheated and plundered
While men stand out in their mess
90   For our world is love, then stress
On the side of our female folks
Men are to cheat without moral checks
What an ugly crippling pot of shame?
In this glaring goof of oppressive game!
But our world divine is an equal world
No human is born only to be abandoned in the cold
Our women have been unjustly chained
In their many roles of mother and . . .
Diana, a victim of incorrigible odds
100   Stands out a martyr of monarchic gods
But Diana sailed the storms to rediscovery
And found herself a new life victory

God bless her royal courage—Princess Diana
The most humane queen never in Britain

7:10 pm
March 13, 1995
Karu, Abuja

ODE TO AN AMERICAN SWALLOW

The dreams to escape from hell to heaven
Has made existence a game of clown and crown
For hardworking young men waste and sicken
In a country where talents frown and drown

Nna had dreams of going to the promise land
Where the vigor of youth could be expensed
Without frustration waving a blindfolding hand
Upon the urge to expire beyond not expressed

A mind to focus as a role model died
10   Leaving some bunch of hopeless lazy thieves
Then the vision of a famous dream he had
Had slowed him down in search of bees in hives

To escape from the jungle for a freedom tell
Has wrung his mind spectra-thin and frail
Then the endless white buffalo hunt spell
Throws a dice in cash and inspiring mail

For to attract a means for the dream escape
Has wrought his mind in the wind and weak
Across many rugged hills of corrupt landscape
20   To merit a man or a woman's kind and meek

Then he swatted after graduation from college
And had the dream of becoming a researcher
In the far away New York Columbia Heights range
The disappointment that came with it is a preacher

And he entered his shell in blank recuperation
Yet to launch another offensive from another point
It occurs that his youthful heart of single attraction
Could serve as a bait to grease his joint

An American Peace Corps Swallow dropped from the blues
30   He nursed her to her knees standing again
He pried into her heart without any clues
She was greatly overwhelmed as how much rain

Of love could really fall from an African heart
The ebony current was too hot indeed for her
She refused to love for the sake of bait
Of flowers, bags, frames, maps, poems, and far

But stung by beauty and youth he searched for love
The swallow was surprised, amused, and indifferent
Left cold chills running down his youthful glove
40   He swallowed his pride, lost his money, and left

The Swallow has gold shiny blonde down her back
Rolling out from beauty springs and face
Sweeping him off his feet to seek her track
Only to attain the height of polite disgrace

His dreams of wedlock with an American swallow
On whose wings and forked tail's might
Could serve as an easy jet to grow
The formidable wings of Boeing 747 in flight

Upon the sacred soil of the great JFK
50   To kiss the American soil in frank supplication
To the God of the great American Citizen's rank
Bowing down to earth in dream-worship fashion

And then raise his voice to tell the world
That a lifelong dream has today come true

For he could now lie on the rail with bold
And beg the train to please take his due

Having endured like Simeon to the Promised Land
Then his soul could afford to sing River Jordan . . .
And march on to the gate of God's mind
60   Leaving the jungle chimes in peace without lantern

And his dreams and ambition to its greatest heights
For to conceive and bear is a long dream
Living in our world is a dream in our hearts
That goes and comes like a flowing stream

10:30 pm
March 7, 1995
Garki, Abuja

TELL THE WATERFALLS

Tell the ceaseless waterfalls
Tell the ripples of the stream
Tell the goldfish swimming across
Tell the water beetles playing with their mates
Tell the beautiful white foams
Tell the endless water bubbles
Tell the flowing quiet stream
Tell the silent green hills
Tell the innocent passing wind
10   Tell the broad and narrow leaves
Tell the green leaves of grass
That I am in love with a girl
That I love this damsel very dearly
That I am deeply in love with her
That my youthful heart is so lonesome
That I have come out here
Quite a distance from home
To dine with all I can find
That my heart is blue
20   That my thoughts are green and pink
That I am in love with a virgin girl
Who cannot love me back
Because my father lives in a little cottage
With the walls made of red earth mud
And the roof made of some thatch
Please send my message across
Even to the crawling black ants
Tell the colorful ladybirds
Tell the beautiful singing lark

30	Tell the proud peacock
	Tell the cooing holy doves
	Tell the silent boulders of rock
	Tell the waving palm fronds
	Tell the hissing breeze passing across
	Tell the smiling evening sun
	Tell whoever that could listen
	That she cannot return my love
	Because I am the son of a plebeian
	Who lives in a little cottage home
40	My father is a rustic man
	Though hers is a good engineer
	My mother is long dead
	Though her mother is alive and well
	Her mother has read the pages
	Of many countless books
	Which mine never knew about

	I have nothing really on earth to inherit
	I have nothing to call my own
	All around me is nothing but a sea of books
50	Though in me flows the blood of noble genes
	But she argues that she cannot eat noble genes
	That she cannot live in noble genes
	She argues that she wants the flamboyant nobility
	The nobility she can feel for the thrill
	The nobility that may not be transferred
	To the generations yet unborn
	Because my father has no wealth moving on four wheels
	My father cannot afford the moving wheels for me
	After my graduation from college
60	Because my father does not live in a castle
	With the foundation of a Gothic Roman architecture
	Because I am the son of a plebeian
	Because I was born humble
	Though with great and noble genes
	She cannot return my love
	Please tell the singing birds

To sing a love song for me
Tell them to sing to my lonely ears
Tell them to sing me to sleep
70   So that I could forget my sorrows
The sorrows of love not returned
Tell the silent Kubwa Hills
Tell the green maize plants
Tell the innocent leaves of the mango tree
Tell the standing black tree
Tell the brooks running downhill
Tell the white clouds moving eastwards
Tell the brilliant setting sun
Tell the silent bark of trees
80   Tell the weeping waterfalls
Tell the inspiring green Kubwa Hills
Tell the undulating distant hills
Tell the silent waving trees
Tell the speechless green landscape
Tell the senseless stones
Tell even the dry leaves of grass
Tell even Mother Nature herself
That true love no longer exists
That the love in my heart is floating
90   Across the green and romantic countryside
Tell everybody, tell everything, tell all the days
That my heartthrob has gone on a train journey
Leaving me lonely and empty
That the world is an empty place for me
That I have tried to forget my love
But the thought of her spoils my day
Please tell the colorful butterflies
To inform the grasshopper, their friends

That I am in need of a heart to preserve mine
100   That I could not love like the Romeos
That there is no more true love
That our twenty-first-century love
Is a love wrapped in affluence

A love bought with money
A love without true love
A love borne from greed
A love without any foundation
A love of what ones father can afford
A love of what ones mother can show
110   A love centered on vanity
A love of silver and gold
And because I am a poor country boy
Who does not have all it takes
To fall in love like in Beverly Hills
Then I can afford to sleep in the jungle
And dine with the squirrels on treetops
And plead with the innocent doves
To share their nests with me
And because I am the son of a plebeian
120   Who cannot afford the wherewithal
And other ingredients of twenty-first-century love
Then I have no business indeed
To fall in love with the daughter of a chief

2:50 pm
July 29, 1994
Looking down waterfalls
Karu Hills
Abuja

Rumbles In My Heart

Some muse to the only girl in my heart
Yes, to the only girl in my heart
What will I call her name?
Please tell me!
Tell me what should I call her?
Should I call her by her name?
Or should I call her Chichi?
Could I just make it up as Chummy?
But she tells me no nickname seems to fit
10   And then I insist that one should really fit
For if Nma is for the rest of the world
Then her real name is just for me
Just for me alone
For my empty heart
Because I am scared to dabble into the sea
I fear a great deal indeed
First to mention her name
Not because she will not like it
Not because she will decide to love me
20   Not because her friends will not envy her
Not just for the fun of it
For the day I will summon the courage
To call her name, her real name
Then the trees of love will blossom
And yield great fruits of beauty and grace
And the fruits will mature and ripen
And when due, the fruits will fall to
The nobles and plebeians alike
For then my heart will cease to be empty

30   For then the fountains of love will flow
The fountains will flow on and on
And there will be no one to stop them
For then the ripples flowing from my fountain pen
Yes, the waters from my fountains of love
She would drink and drink deeply too
She would drink the water of Ezeiyi Fountains
For then she will become a new person
A brand new virgin princess of Eluama
For then she would have drank from my love fountain
40   And then her eyes could now open
So that she could behold
Yes, her eyes will open to behold
The virgin scenes
Yes, the virgin scenes of the panoramic green Kubwa Hills
For then she could love
She could then start loving
For then her heart will melt
Before my endless fountains of love
For then she will pause for a while
50   And listen to the gods
She will hear the gods saying:

"You sweet little young thing
The uncrowned virgin princes of Eluama
The daughter of a chief—his royal highness
The dame whose name rings a bell
And reverberates an endless echo from green Kubwa Hills
The girl whose name brings good luck
The girl whose name is sweet to the ears
The girl whose lips are soft and pink
60   The girl whose eyes cast a shadow of rainbow
The only ripple in a man's heart
The only girl in a man's heart
The only girl whose name means love
My dear virgin princess of Eluama
Listen to the wisdom of the old
The wisdom of the gods as they are

It may appear that his humble roots
Scares your youthfulness, but take note
That many nobles were born humble
70   In mouse-hole cottages
With gaping and ragged yawning roofs
For nobles do not grow from the earth like carrots
Nobles are made before nobles are born

So many are born noble
With smooth spotless skin
But a few like him achieved nobility
With some scars here
And some scars there

You may pretend never to love
80   You may pretend not to have a heart
Your love may have been suppressed
And forced to fade away into the hills
But the acclaimed universal truth
Is that you are human made of flesh and blood
And that whenever you are ready to love
His hands will be spread wide apart
To welcome you home to his Lilies
Because the truth remains
That only he could have loved you
90   Like the love in the petals of rose
Only he could have loved you
From the true heart of love
A love you can count on
A love without regrets

For he is not ashamed of loving a girl
Who cannot love him back
For he will rather drown himself
In sweet fountain pools of love
And take joy in telling the world
100   About his endless love for you

Than to die alone at home in silence
With all the load pining endlessly
In his firebrand lovesick heart

Remember, that there is nothing you can do
To convince him about how much you despise him
For despite all your attempts
Despite all your denials
They precipitate one thing
They spin some endless love webs
110   From the cloacae of a restless love spider
For they spin out more and more love webs
From his restless love fountain pen

Let the secret be made known
To the entire human world that even if
You were married to an African prince tomorrow
And somehow you realized your folly
And got a separation from the prince
His arms will still be wide open
To welcome the remains of you
120   Because his love for you could never die

For if you were a virgin apple
Dropped into his sweating lovesick palms
He will sure keep you ever fresh
He will keep you ever dew-drop fresh
He will tend to you as his love garden
For he will kiss your lips wet all the time
For he will massage your back and bones
For he will caress your chest and belly
For he will kiss your sensuous virgin lips
130   For he will sweep you off your feet
And then drop you on a bed of love
Made of nothing but the smoothness of fine fabrics
The finest fabrics of cotton and silk
And he will feed you from the fountains of love
And then you will roar in ecstasy like the waves

Being carried up and down her currents
And you will moan and shed tears of love
For he will tickle the sole of your feet
For he will play in the small of your back
140   For he will drown in the small of your fronts
For he will smother you with love
For he will love you in a manner
You have never been made to love before
For he will pour on you some love
The kind of love you have never felt
Lifting you away into space
Where nothing else mattered
Except the exploits of long awaited love
For he will love you in a way
150   You have never been made to imagine before
For then he would have succeeded
In ferrying you across to the island of love
Where you could never ever ask for more
For he is a celebrated lover boy
Who will tend to your love gardens
All the days of his mortal life

Though you may be pretty young
Though you may be quite inexperienced
Though you may be really naïve
160   Though you may be the virgin princess
Yes, the virgin princess of Eluama
Though whatever you may be
Never allow age and parental desires
To becloud your youthful sense of judgment
More importantly when it has to do with love
For your own real love
Is only one in the world
And he is there eager to ferry you
Across to your own island of love

170   For if you have ever dreamt of something
Something so dear to your virgin heart

Which of course you cannot get
Then you are a little close to the way
Yes, the way, the truth about the way
He thinks and feels about you

For if you could read his mind
Then you could write volumes and volumes
About the yearnings of his lovesick heart
And then you can open your inner minds
180   And confess to the whole world about some truth
Yes, some truth, some frank truth
About how your love for him was suppressed

For if you could muster the courage
To explore the blades of his petals of rose
Then they will sure give you
Some finer details, yes, some finer points
About his great love for you
For if you were the daughter of a plebeian
And he is the prince of Eluama
190   And you happen to fall in love with him
But it appears he could not return your love
Because his father—the King discouraged him
Then you will sure experience exactly how it feels
To love somebody who can't love you back

For if you believe that people
Do not fall in love with their pen
Then it is high time you realize
That the fire of the candle flame of most love affairs
Are enkindled and sustained for endless times
200   With the melting wax of a lover's fountain pen

'My dear virgin princess of Eluama
My dear Nma
My dear sweet heart
My dear honey
My dear sweety!

My endless heartthrob
My darling petals of rose'

"You could hear him cry for love
For if you could be brave enough
210   To give him your idea of a home
For you to live in with him
Then he could summon his architect
To make a model of a home
First, before mustering the courage
To gather some rock here
And some pebbles there
For the foundation stone
Of your dream home
Yes, your dream home where Lilies grow
220   And leaves of grass sing some endless rhymes."

8:45 am
October 30, 1994
Karu FHA Estate
Abuja

ASK THE QUEEN OF LOVE

On this day the wind of events
Brought me into the lobby
Of the prestigious Nicon Noga Hilton Abuja
And here in one corner
I did find myself isolated
Four steps below the entrance level
In a crescent-shaped garden sitting area
In my own little world
With a mild orange glow
10   From an anthill-shaped fireplace
Emitting some romantic shade of orange light
Like the glow of lovers candlelight dinner
Which illuminates my scribbling diary
Here the milieu interior is quite temperate
The glass walls are dazzling
Splashing jet of the water fountains
Amaze the cross beams of light
Creating a crisscross of rainbow fountains
While the leaves of grass
20   With endless dew drops clap their hands ceaselessly
And also sing some endless love songs
The Jazz music from the Capital Bar
Soothes my worn out nerves to use
And even some strokes of the violin
From the Berlin Philharmonic Orchestra
Of the Mozart's composition
Leaves me in an ideal creative world
Where some leaves of trees hanging above my forehead
Create their own inspirational niche

30   And as I sit here looking
Out of the proximity
Of Mother Nature herself
In these glass walls with jungle twines
Though all these make their own impressions
But all that preoccupies my mind
Is how much emptiness that exists in my heart
For I wished greatly that Nma
Is sitting here next to me
I wished she is here looking into my eyes
40   Holding my hands while we steal a kiss or two
I wished she is here telling me a story
Calling my sweet name
And even polishing it with interludes of "my dear"
I wished we could share some Chapman
Yes, some Hilton Chapman laced with lemon juice
While we watch the dazzling drills
Of the ceaseless water fountains
And whisper into each other's ears
Some sweet little talks
50   Some sweet nothings
Whispering about love and sweetness of love
For I wished we could walk down to the pool
And take one headlong plunge or two
Into the pool, and then we can play with water
She could splash water on my face and giggle
While I gasp for air and swim away
Then swim to the floor of the pool
And then pull her on her big toe
While she screams in fright
60   And I swim to the surface
And laugh at her till my lungs ached
And we could also take a walk side by side
And visit the handicraft center
Where I could buy some bangles
Made of ivory from elephant tusks
I would buy a little bag for her
Which she could hang on her shoulder

While we walked on the grass lawns
With our bare feet kissing the green grass
70   But all these are mere dreams
For I sincerely miss this girl very dearly
For here I closed my eyes and dreamt dreams
And even more and more I miss my little queen
For I really do miss her to a point of tears
Yes, some diamond tears dropping down my eyes
But while I meditate
One wholesome thought crept into me
"Why do you miss her so much?
While she may never have remembered your name
80   Why do you miss her so much?
While she has chosen to go out with some other guy
Why do you miss her so much?
While she has chosen to date someone else
Yes, to follow another man
Who may even be slapping her face?
And rupturing her virgin hymen?
And she will rather laugh aloud in ecstasy
Than show any sign that she is hurt
Because she doesn't want to lose him
90   Because she sees him as her love idol
Because she sees him as her sex symbol
Because she sees him as her Prince Charming
Who makes her pants wet
By mere sight of his masculine figure
For she may be worshipping him
As her own idol superstar
The only man in her life
The only guy who knows well
What love really means to her
100   Meanwhile you are here dying in isolation
Thinking and missing a girl
Who does not give a damn
Whether you are dead or alive
The girl you call your little queen
The girl you call your own angel

The girl that is endowed with all your dreams of love
Yes, all the qualities you dream of in a woman
The girl who fits into the perfect lost shoe
Yes, into the perfect lost shoe of Cinderella
110   The voice which coos like the doves'
The girl whose skin is fair and ebony
The girl whose father is a King
The girl whose mother is an intellectual
Yes, she is the only girl in your life
And perhaps the only girl in the world?
You better grow up young man
And explore the world of dames
And then push your finger around
And find yourself a girl
120   And find your real heartthrob wherever she is"

But I pine every other day
Missing this girl like I miss my mum
And sad enough when I tried to forget her
My creative inspirations ceased to flow
And I went into creative hibernation
But when the thought of her rebounded
The inspirations were pouring
The inspirations were pouring like rain
For this is the greatest of my heart desire
130   For this is what I want to dream about
For the inspirations give me the confidence
For the inspirations give me joy
For the inspirations restore my towering ego
And reassure me of the man I dream of myself
For the inspirations propel me to the mountain clouds
Yes, the inspirations make me do
Just about the only thing I love to do
For I have always dreamt great dreams
To write without restraint
140   For I will rather want to see myself
As a lovesick bird
So that I can keep pouring out my lines

So that I can keep singing of love
For when they cease to pour
For when the muse cease to regenerate
I am very depressed and moody
And Nma is an inspirational muse symbol
And Nma sweeps out these songs of love
From my volatile subconscious
150 And they keep pouring on and on
They pour like rain and overwhelm me
And I plead with the queen of love
To give me the heart of Nma
So that I could keep it only for myself
For as long as I live
So that I could sustain these inspirations
So that they could keep coming
Yes, so that they will keep falling like rain
For I have always wondered
160 Why many a time no muse crosses my path
And sometimes emotions laden inspirations
Sweep me away in high currents
And endlessly I question myself
What can I do to win her heart?
Where can I go to get the answers?
Who could I ask to help me?
Where on earth could I get some help?
For it seems to me I cannot live without her
I cannot sleep without her it seems
170 I want her to bear my children
I want her to call me dear
I want her to cook my meals
I want her to nurse me when am ill
I want to be her superstar
I want to be the only man in her life
I frankly do not know
Yes, I do not know what to do
For I am somewhat lost
For when I ask my friends

180   They get irritated and envious
About how much I could love
And they ask me to sort it out myself
They tell me to solve the riddle in my own way
But I do not know how to crack the nut
And when I insist on an answer
One of them told me to go
To the hills of muse in the green Kubwa Hills
Atop the peak of green Kubwa Hills
And question the Queen of Love

8:45 pm
October 31, 1994
Lobby, Nicon Noga Hilton Abuja

PLEASE TAKE OVER ME

I have slept many times
And woke up many times too
But each time there is only one person
Yes, there is one person in my mind
And I am sure you need not be told
Because you have heard her name
Over and over, again and again
For the truth remains that she drives me crazy
Her name is Nma, an eighteen-year-old virgin princess
10   The candid truth is that she makes tears flow
Yes, she evokes tears to flow out of my eyes
While I plead for her to return my love
For many times I do not only feel like crying
I actually see tears flowing down my eyes
I found myself in love ecstasy, squeezing my pillow
Wetting my pillow case with tears of love
While I plead and ask Nma to return my love
Because I am in love with her
But she does not understand me
20   And I am swept off my feet
By the beauty and elegance in her eyes
Some say that I should leave her alone
That when she grows up she will listen
That she does not love me
That she is rather in love with someone else
Some others think she is shy
And that she cannot show up now
Because she is much younger than myself
Still so many others believe

30 That I should let her loose into the winds
  That if she is mine that she will come back
  Others say I should give her time to grow up
  And then go back to her
  Some others feel that her parents
  Are influencing her mood and reaction
  Because she is the only girl in the family
  Others say leave her alone
  "When she has fallen in love once
  And her heart is broken twice
40 She will run and run looking for you"
  Knowing too well that my love for her
  Will still be alive like a candle flame
  Most others are rather cautious
  And they advise me to be careful
  As I may experience the worst heartbreak
  If I should spend the rest of my life
  With a woman who does not really love me
  But right inside me in my subconscious

  I have this overwhelming conviction
50 That despite everything Nma will come back
  She will one day come back looking for me
  For she knows that there is no one else
  Who could love her like I have professed?
  Though my friends tell me
  To rather keep the girl who is crazy about me
  Than the one who will give me a heart attack
  And I am so confused and in a dilemma
  For I do not know what to do
  I have a girl who loves me very dearly
60 I am her greatest source of inspiration
  And I have inspired her to write a book
  Yes, my frank dedication to our friendship
  Has crystallized in her subconscious as an idol
  And she writes endlessly out of my inspiration
  And when she writes her storybook
  She prefers to use my name as the title of the book

And she goes a step further
And dedicates the book to me
She is doing all these in the name of love
70   She does all these just for the sake of love
She believes in me
She adores me
Though I am a mortal, but she idolizes me
She loves to hear me read my poems
While she makes herself comfortable on my chest
She believes I am a superstar
And she writes me letters every fortnight
She misses me dearly many a time
And whenever she sees me she melts
80   Yes, she melts on my arms like snow
For she is as pretty as the snow drops
And I call her my snow girl
She is tall and quite elegant too
And she is fair with a lot of hair
She is intelligent to a point of creativity
And she loves me so much
That sometimes she even cries
While she lays on my arms
She coos my name with softness
90   She washes my clothes without being told
She knows when am hungry
She knows my best dishes too
She buys my best fruits when she visits
I could see the color of love in her eyes
She is working hard to win my heart
She knows nearly every story
Behind the scars on my leg
And she does not mind the scars
As they make me less a Prince Charming
100   She watches over me sometimes when I sleep
And she loves to hear me sing
And even make a rap song from my poems
She is worried when I am distressed
And she even prays for me

Each time I confide my problems to her
She wants to be the mother of my children
She tells me she will like to play mum
And I will play her son
And she even treats me like one
110   For she designed and sewed a T-shirt for me
She is the only person in the world
Who has ever remembered my birthday
And even went ahead to buy a birthday card for me
For others are only interested in my remembering theirs
In reality she actually plays mother
And sometimes she is tempted
Yes, she is tempted to bath me
Just like a mother does to a son
Though I am not a baby anymore
120   But then she actually rubs powder on my face
And when she calls my name
I hear the echo of the love lark
Rolling down from the peak of the green Kubwa Hills
And I feel a cold chill run down my spine
For I am scared of not exchanging rings with her
For she will be my ideal wife
For she will be my mother too
And also the sweet mother of my children
But whenever I remember that
130   I could feel a stream of tears
Gather at the other side of my brain
And I do not know what to do
And once when she looked deeply into my eyes
She could see Nma bluffing at my pleas
Saying things like "No, not him again"
And my girl burst out crying
And when I ask her why she is crying
She asks me whether I don't know the reason
And her diamond tears drop down my shoulders
140   As she weeps endlessly for love
And I call them the tears of true love
But I have severally wondered

How on this planet does she know?
For when my love for her drowned
Was a time she wronged me
And shattered the bedrock of our love
And it was within that long interval
That I saw Nma for the first time
And I willingly fell in love with her
150   And I also stupidly gave my heart to her
And now Nma has taken my heart
And my girl is pleading to have it back
But the task is enormous, truly herculian
Because I have fallen head over heels in love
Though heightened by an atonement for her deeds
And I cannot pour all my love accolades on her
For I have rather preferred to choose the wind—Nma
Yes, chasing the perfection in a virgin
Yes, her virginity is the diamond mine
160   Which spur my inspirations to the clouds
For I do wonder and question myself
What if I learnt that she is no more a virgin?
How could that affect all this perfectionist dedication?
But I will rather not want to imagine that
Because I do enjoy the poetic celebration while it lasts
But at my quiet moments
I do greatly question myself
Who is this queen called love?
And why is she so partial and powerful?
170   Why is she so uncompromising?
Why does she cherish a suffering state?
Just to be allowed into her dream bosom
Who is this enigmatic queen called love?
And what will I do?
For I do not know
For I do not want to cause a heartbreak
And yet I cannot let go
My endless, secret love for Nma
For my girl senses the aura of Nma

180   Hovering around my subconscious
From deep down her heart
But she will rather keep me to herself
And pray that things turn out good tomorrow
To her own gentle favor
For she would prefer that Nma
Takes all the love in poetic celebration
And she gets the real thing
And she gets her dream man of love
And keeps him to her bosom all her life
190   But I schooled my little head and wondered
How I could fall so deeply in love?
With a girl who has not tasted the water of love
How could I afford to roast my heart?
For the rest of my life
Just for the sake of the crush of love?
How could I accept to be kicked around?
Instead of the glamour of being pampered
Yes, the glamour of being pampered like a son
One great thing I have missed all my life
200   How could I continue to crave for the wind?
For I miss all the care and dedication of true love
As a compensation for receiving this love
Yes, for experiencing this illusive love
And everything causes me some pain
For if I do tell anyone
That I'd not love my girl
Then I am one big liar
But to accept her before a priest
Is yet another kettle of fish
210   And where Nma kicks me out
At the end of this day of love
Long after my sweetheart
Has found solace in another man's arms
Will eventually leave me in the cold
Without anyone to love me like mother
And so what is my best option?

'For many say take the devil you know
And forget the angel you don't know'
But my heart is empty
220   With the devil I do know
And I will rather prefer to accept the angel
Yes, the angel I do not know at all
And I seem more confused every day
And when I bother my friends too much
They asked me to questions the Queen of Love
That maybe she may have an answer
But I frankly do not know what to do
And I plead with the Queen of Love
To take over me
230   And rule my mortal love life
In these endless puzzles about love
For I am confused even more and more

7:35 pm
October 31, 1994
Lobby, Nicon Noga Hilton Abuja

TELL THE BEAUTY OF AFRICAN WOMEN

As a child in the country hills of Eluama
Learning about the rudiments of life's banner
I rose up one morning with the awakening surprise
To the reality that I have never seen the sunrise
And I questioned my dad about my mum
He looks at the ceiling with clouds of rum
Pleading with me to persevere for a little while
Then he took me back to my dream file
To an orchestration by the cream of African women
10   An enviable galaxy of bright African peahens
With the eagle's eye of childhood and innocence
I beheld my mum and her likes in elegance

Then I saw tears come down my innocent eyes
They were tears of joy and mix feelings in disguise
I listened with rapt attention as the songs rain
In festivity to the elegance of a beauty train
Educating me about mum and other African women
I saw myself hilariously withdrawn from men
Listening to the inspiring songs of African beauty
20   Falling endlessly from the mountains of festivity
Singing this African song of love . . .

Tell me about the beauty of African women
For the beauty of their skin makes the doves coo
For their immaculate white teeth melt the Swiss snow
For their charming eyeballs reign in beauty train
For their black hair is a blessing to humanity

For their dark skin glitter in the morning sun
And their beautiful faces shine as bright as the peahens
Tell it to the hills and mountains of Africa
Tell it to the lowland and rift valleys of East Africa
Tell it to the soft green hills of Nsukka
Tell it to the plains and plateau of Jos
Tell the singing trees and laughing rocks
Tell the muse-laden hills and valleys of Eluama
Tell the rising sun from the east of the Niger
Tell the puppies in the white clouds of Africa
Tell even the pebbles and the leaves of grass
Tell me about the beauty of African women
So that I could well educate other peoples

Tell me about the intoxicating charm of the Somali girl
Singing her songs of beauty in the horn of Africa
Tell Aroma, my virgin African beauty
To please sing me a song of love
Tell me about the overwhelming beauty gem
Of the African American dames and their likes
In all the Caribbean Islands and also far and wide
Tell me about the beauty of the Igbo girl
Tell me about the charm of the Hausa girl
Tell me about the elegance of the Yoruba girl
Please tell me about the elegance and beauty of my mother
Tell me about her brown and romantic eyeballs
Tell me about her charming round face
Tell me about her shining black hair
Tell me about the African Beauty Queen at School
Tell me about the beauty of the Fulani girl
Tell me about the beauty of the Basotho women
Tell me about the beauty of Winnie at fifty
For the skin of an aging African woman never wrinkles
Tell me about the beauty of the African Song Bird
Yes, tell me about Maria Makeba of blessed memory
Tell me about the snow drops of Egyptian Cleopatra
Tell me about the charm of the Ashanti girl
Sing me the songs of the beauty of all African women

Have you beheld the charm of the East African Women?
How about the beauty of Ngwa Nma of Eluama
Have you seen ebony beauty dressed in ivory beads?
Sing me the songs of the beauty of African women
Tell me the tales of the elegance of African beauty
Go to the African universities in Nigeria and Kenya
And behold the black beauty of African girls
70   As they pour out from their lecture halls
Clutching their books and bags in beauty throngs
Looking like the little angels in their groups
Walking gracefully with an African pride
Go to Jos terminus and behold the masterpiece
Yes, the statue of African beauty
Radiating her African beauty with enduring pride
Tell the beauty of African women

Tell it to the Mambila highlands and Cameroon Mountains
Tell it to the waterfalls in Ezeiyi Fountains
80   Tell it to the mountains of Kilimanjaro
Tell it to the wild hills of Ekpeke
Tell it to the hills and mountains of Africa
Tell it to the hot springs of Yankari
Tell it to the singing waves of the Atlantic
That there are beauty springs flowing here
Yes, beauty springs flowing here in Africa
From the White Nile to the Blue Nile
Flowing down into the Mediterranean Sea
90   From the Niger and Benue to the Atlantics
Flowing across through the Bight of Biafra
Where the Igbo woman embraced her beauty
From the waters of Rivers Senegal to that of Congo
Did very many African women embrace African beauty!
From River Orange to River Limpopo
Did the Basotho and Zulu women acquire beauty!
From River Zambezi to the Atlantic Ocean
From Victoria Falls to the Ezeiyi Fountains
Did African beauty springs shower the daughters of Africa!

100   From all these great rivers of Africa
       From all these great waters of Africa
       Have the beauty of African woman
       Been polished to a point of perfection

       Tell me the tales of African beauty
       Sing me the songs of the African beauty
       So that the African man will love with pride
       So that the African woman will know her great worth
       For beauty was first born here in Africa
       Before it diffused generously to other continents
110   Yes, here in the hills and valleys of Africa
       Yes, here in the plains and plateau of Africa
       Yes, here in the rivers and lakes of Africa
       Did endless beauty springs flow in ripples
       Flowing and flowing endlessly across the Sahara
       Watering the sand dunes from the Nile to Cape Town
       Singing these great songs of love about African beauty
       With infinite beauty heritage pouring out from our genes
       Celebrating the beauty of African women with pride

       8:45 am
       December 29, 1995
       Wuse Park
       Abuja

ODE TO MONIC

Tell Monic that I could not sleep last night
Tell her that sleep eluded me
Though I wished greatly I could fall asleep
Tell her that I remember her a great deal
That I have welded diverse imaginations
About what a lovely girl she might be
Tell her that I love her more
Than she could really imagine
Tell her that the reasons for my love
10   Are truly in multiple dimensions
That my auntie did tell me a great deal
Yes, a great deal about her
That auntie talks a great deal about her
Tell Monic that Auntie loves her too
And that she represents a soft spot
In my auntie's subconscious
And that I do confess of being infected
To a point of dedication to love her
Tell that when I saw Echi's album
20   During her summer vacation in a Mexican Coast
That the beauty I beheld sends waves down me
Tell her that I am a pilot though
But that I have this knack for writing
And that because she has been in my mind
All through the day and night too
I could not resist the urge but to write
To feast on her beauty in poetic celebration

Tell her that her pictures I saw
Revealed many qualities I greatly admire
30   That her height drives me a little crazy
Tell Monic that her beautiful face
Is indeed a blessing to the human race
Tell her that I sincerely do send my love
And that what my auntie says about her
Greatly points to her instinctive subconscious search
For her missing roots back home in Africa
Tell Monic that we in Africa love her too
Just as much as we love Echi and Didi
Tell her that her tasty buds
40   For African dishes is an indirect invitation
For her to visit us here in Africa
To her real roots just like Alex Haley
To acquaint herself with her roots in Africa
Tell her that her love of African costumes
Though living thousands of miles away in the New World
Is indeed a true testimony to the origin of her roots
Tell Monic that the elegance of her beauty
Makes my heart beat a little faster
Giving me sleepless and restless nights
Making me toss around my bed
50   From left to right
And from length to breadth
Questioning my lovesick self
"Why are you so much in love?
With a girl whom you don't know?
Are you not infatuated young man?"
But my subconscious fights back in defense
"That there is no harm in loving anyone
As there is in hating someone
For love is a natural universal phenomenon
60   Cutting across all geographical and ethnic barriers
Unlike hatred which hatches into wars and chaos"
For then I mustered enough courage
Yes, enough will force to bare my mind

To tell Monic that I am on vacation
And that I have all the time in the world
To point out for her a clear picture of herself
From the eagle's eye of a falcon crest
And then sing my endless songs of love . . .
TELL Monic . . .
70   My crystal of an African-American beauty
That she is making me a little crazy
Keeping me sleepless in poetic creativity
Making my golden pen go greasy
Tell my dear snowdrop Monic
That from the songs of an African love lark
I did see her shining in the beauty park
Reflecting from her charming pictures
Revealing many hidden love treasures
Where her snow-white teeth
80   Wake the sleeping doves from their nests
Dazzling like a piece of diamond
Revealing some tenderly nurtured almond
With her rosy cheeks uncovering an alpha-buster
While her glassy eyes twinkle like the morning star
Radiating an IQ of profound magnitude
Offering her a seat in an American medical school
For her long hair, shiny and beauty bound
Has kept me captive on a beauty stool
With her skin glittering like the Mexican beach
90   Extolling great potential in this African-American princess
For her dimpled neck is a beauty crown to reach
By any bard who knows her worth beyond her grin
Ferrying her along to her dream island of love
Where she could get more than her bargain
Propelling her to the mountain clouds above
Snowing with beads of love than she could retain
Keeping her in one piece without any regret
When her long romantic legs could reach out for more
To enkindle a new fire of love with a clarinet

100   Which will glow with gladness and splendor
For an expected celebration of this pot of gold
Weighing beautifully in my scale of pearls
Where beauty springs sing some rhymes in the cold
Sweeping her juicy lips in ecstasy of love meals

3:00 am
January 11, 1995
19 Kamsalem Road
Malali
Kaduna

Ode To Naomi Campbell

Have you ever seen a black swan?
Flying gracefully across many country lakes
Have you ever seen an ebony cloud tan?
Making rainbow drops fall like moon light flakes
Have you sat on a rock beside Lake Victoria?
And sing like a lark holding the world spell bound
For her dazzling white teeth cast a golden mound
Of the glorious African setting sun
Oh, Naomi! Crystal of beauty in a model spoon

10   Have you seen a sweet swallow smile?
Flying across full of fun free for all
Telling a tale with pride in ebony beauty and style
Thrilling first-class magazines standing tall
When her supple chocolate skin sings endless songs of love
Throwing millionaires unconsciously overboard their yacht
Her glittering long hair transmits heat without a stove
And leave many in wet dreams and pasty patch
Her strawberry eyes are a virgin love jungle
While her thin silky eyelashes is a nest for a pelican
20   Then her chiseled ivory nose causes a rumble
Her honey coated lips are dew drops on a beauty pan

Oh, Naomi! You were molded when God was ready and fresh
For he took his time to blend the curves and contours
The hands and legs were made to wield enormous cash
Then the long but apple-size face leaves no flaws
But then her graceful model's catwalk is rich
To the tune of large fortunes smiling on her face

For on Naomi's beauty many million dollars stretch
And leave wealthy men bidding from eternity to space
30   Naomi is a watershed where beauty and modeling mate
Turning the world around in her fingers to her taste
For on her creamy smiles many African larks hum
For in her dreamy eyes ripens many a love plum

For her youthfulness and the life in her eyes
Melts a snowcapped mountain of Kilimanjaro
The skin-creased dimples on her neck is a spice
To the elegance and smoothness of this African swallow
For her heron gait makes the Kenyan safari jealous
While the perfection of her beauty curves
40   Have thrown many of her rivals into spigots
For Naomi is just nothing but a pack of beauty balls
Naomi is a girl as good a human as gold
For she is just a sample of the future African banner
Watch out for the twenty-first-century Naomis in Africa
Will someday fill the pot with African content

For the exploits of Naomi and black Africa in diaspora
Will someday reveal the richness of Mother Africa
And then carve a niche
For all Africans to reach
50   Tell Naomi she makes my eyes wet
And that I cannot any longer wait
To behold in its true colors
The flawless magnificence of her beauty claws

10:30 am
April 4, 1995
Karu, Abuja

WHEN THE FOUNTAINS
OF LOVE HAVE DRIED

Nma
The virgin princess of Eluama
When will you learn to love?
When will you fall in love?
Like every other person does
When will your heart learn to love?
Like all other human hearts do
When will you learn to love?
Someone back, for the sake of love?
10   When will your heart soften?
And then respond to the songs of love
Well, maybe when you get old
Maybe when you lose your charm
Maybe when you grow up to love
Maybe when you realize your ambitions
Maybe when age catches up with you
Maybe when you will be a lonely old woman
Maybe when you fall into the wrong hands
Maybe when you love someone dearly
20   Who has no atom of love for you?
Maybe when the moon stays behind
And refuses to spread its ineffectual beams
Maybe when the sun goes to an endless sleep
And throws Planet Earth into an endless darkness
Maybe when the birds stop tweeting
Their endless love tweets while lovers search
Maybe when the virgins on green Kubwa Hills
Would have lost their charm of purity

Maybe when the queen of the Kubwa Hills
30   Will decide to desert the virgin princesses
Maybe when beautiful princesses like you
Will cease to be born in the Hills of Eluama
Maybe when the Elegant Daughters of Eluama
Will no longer be born to marry
The illustrious sons of Eluama
Maybe then when the sun sets
Down the valley of Nkoji-Ala
Maybe when the sun refuses to rise
From the peak of the East of green Kubwa Hills
40   Maybe when the cock crows
At a moment it loses its crown
Maybe, when the cock never crows at all
To the dawn of a new era of love
Maybe then when true love would have died
Maybe then when your heart has been broken
Many times in the endless search for true love
Maybe then when you would have been bashed
Left, right, and center in the name of love
This is fake and untrue unlike mine
50   Maybe then when your heartthrob will frown
Each time he sees your face in the crowd
Maybe then when people no longer fall in love
Maybe then when the love of purity and innocence
Would have died a slow and painful death
In the minds of men and women who cherish it
Maybe then when no one writes poems
For the lucky elegant virgin princess of Eluama
Maybe then when mushrooms
Will cease to grow on the plains
60   And the undulating beautiful hills
Of my endless inspiration Eluama
Maybe then when the beautiful ones
Have lived and died in frustration
Maybe then when the heart beat
For the impulse of a heart in love
Will cease to pound away in excitement

At the mere sight of a loved one
Maybe when the petals of rose
Will no longer grow in the Lilies
70   Maybe then when there will be no more
Tears of joy from falling in love
To someone who understand the meaning of love
When the beauty of the petals of rose
Could not any more stir my fountain pen?
When the love of petals of rose
Will have faded away in the memories of time?
When there will be nothing like love anymore?
When the immortal goddess of love will expire?
When there will be no more immortality?
80   When love will become a mortal entity?
When all will expire without meaning?
When the winds of love in Eluama
Will cease to blow our innocent hearts
When young men will no more fall in love
And all the young women will starve in loneliness
When the excitement of youth will end
When the illustrious sons of Eluama
Will cease to marry the elegant daughters
When the pure spring waters from Ezeiyi
90   Will no longer bubble as it does
When the beauty of Adaoma Hills
Will not anymore activate my muse
When I could have ceased to exist
And I will take solace in flying with the wind
When no more inspirations come out of me
When life itself will come to a halt
And the leaves of grass will cease to be green
Then the crescent green Kubwa Hills
Would have faded away in isolation
100   And the endless muse they create will be no more
When all the springs of love will dry up
When the fountains of love have dried
When the endless streams of love
Will no more be important to our use

And life will have no more meaning
As the mortal man cannot live without love
Then when all that have been said
May have been done in their order
Then when the leaves of grass
110 No longer sing beautiful love songs
When the trees will cease to dance
Their daily dance of the forest
As the winds of time play their tunes
When the golden sands of the beach
Will vanish into the thin air
When the cool breeze from the valleys
Will cease to caress our hearts
When nature herself will cease to be romantic
When memories of the innocence
120 And the purity of childhood
Will no more haunt my muse
When the beauty of the Lilies
In Lake Adaoma will shade their charms
When all the waterfalls will stand still
When the rains of love will cease to fall
When the lakes of love will dry up
And leave the love birds on dry land
When the cold of Harmattan
Will no longer chill the bones of men
130 And help others sleep all night
Coiled up like babies in the warmth
Of their love-laden blankets
When the rocks are no more romantic
When the human face of Zuma Rock
Will have been lost to time
By the ugly agents of love denudation
When the agents of love denudation
Will change the topography of the earth
And scrape off the word "Love"
140 From the vocabulary of all languages
Such that humans with the heart to love
Cannot anymore thrive in one piece

And they would all fall asleep quietly
Hoping to awaken again
Maybe when your heart may have
Realized its folly in its actions
For then the ripples in the brook will sing
Their never ending songs of love
To their sweethearts the pebbles
150   Yes, the pebbles at the bottom of the brooks
When the beauty of my muse—Eluama
Will be no more in my memories
When the petals from my red roses
Would have all fallen off in isolation
And withered away unnoticed
When hens will no more lay eggs
When the geese will cease to lay golden eggs
When horses will no more have hooves
And mortals will live without hearts
160   Then you could know how bitter it could be
To love someone very dearly
Who never appreciates what it means to love
For even a day old baby loves
From the heart of love
For even the puppies love their mother
For even the cubs love their fellows
For even the baby doves learn to love
Then why not you—a teenage princess
For when the wind of love will cease to blow
170   To you in any direction at all
Maybe then you will rediscover the joy
In loving someone who cares for you
And by then you would have felt the sadness
There is, that exists in the emptiness
In loving someone
Who never loves you back
In loving someone
Who frowns his face
When he sees you

180   Even the beauty in your princessly face
          Never stirs any nerve ending
          Then you learn the hard way
          The agony and the distress
          Of falling in love with a wall
          A senseless rigid unromantic wall
          Which stands there all day and all night
          Which never utters a word
          Which never ever calls your name
          Maybe then when there is no one to love
190   No one to fall in love with
          Then the love center in your brain
          Will have been reactivated
          To love the emptiness
          In a lonesome world
          Where all the springs of love
          Have all dried up in frustration
          And there will be no one for you
          Just no one for your mortal self
          To love and cherish to the end
200   Who will sing the songs of love
          To your immortal lovesick heart!

11:05 am
January 12, 1994
Abuja Clinics Ltd.
Karu, Abuja

UNSEALED
LOVE LETTERS

TODAY IS YOUR BIRTHDAY

DEAR NMA I

I am searching for you
Down the Atlantic shores today
Though I know too well
That today is your birthday
For I could not write
Nor attend to share your day
For you have not handed me
The baton for the relay
For your "more important visitors"
May have taken their place
In the great portions of your heart
And the juicy space
Of your treasured islands
Which have haunted me of late
Applying myself to its fullest
To prepare a tent in the state
For you and for me
To put our heads when it rains
And learn to take each other along
On time to enable us to catch the trains
I can see the sea, the waves
And the storm in their mists
In the turbulent sea in twists
For I only saw your shadow
Walking in the angry sea
Not really touched
By the lonesome lost key

To the treasured locks
Which could open the gates of my life
30 And lead me into a new world
Without any more strife
I am standing beside the roaring seas
Watching the waves grow like monstrous trees
Though the sea is alive and busy at war with herself
I am lost in thoughts without you in myself
For in the rise and fall of the innocent waves
I see you tossed here and there in the waves
Of the white giant ripples rising and falling
I stretch my hands to touch you but nothing
40 There was nothing but the empty shore and beach
I asked myself where could I go?
"When would I reach?"
To tell you how much
My heart yearns for you
My corporate being
The self in me
The real me too
Long for you
Your elegant self
50 My rare gem
For I know that you are young
That you are young at heart like a stem
Supple, fragile, and pretty
And an ambitious young girl
For I am certain that you know
That you know my real style
For I happened to be born ambitious too
With a volcanic zeal to succeed
For I am empty and helpless
60 Without your beautiful seed
For I feel the tears of my emptiness
Flowing down my cheeks
For I do know that you are nuts
The only pretty girl in the creeks
The truth though is that love counts

For I love you with all the nerve endings
In me, stretching from my busy brain
To many more things
On which life itself rests
70   As we helpless and blind mortals
Grope in the dark in search
Of endless things in rituals
Charging like the rhino
To a harmless stump of wood
For I dream of when you could
Read my thoughts and mood
And learn to lend me a hand
And share my warmth
For I dream of when you could
80   Wipe the tears of growth
And rescue me from the lonesomeness
With the muse of the luring sea goddess
For I dream when we could
Share my pen and goodness
And read the lines that flow
In chorus from my thoughts
For I dream of when we will
Explore the sea like a twin
And listen to the muse
90   Of the sea rise and fall
Like in the womb
Where we rolled like a ball
My mind longs for your pond
Two of us in our balloon
Though I find myself
Lonesome in my cocoon
My heart is heavy like the clouds
My head is cloudy like the mounds
As I watch the roaring wave of the sea
100   Though I don't know what I see
I stretch my imaginations with the waves
But I know not where to begin, and end
For I find myself helplessly in love

Without your treasured trendy glove
Or how to console our lonesome minds
Crying helplessly to the Venus of the winds
Your love,

10:00 am
August 28, 1993
Beside the shore of the
Atlantic Ocean, Tarkwa Bay, Lagos

I Cannot Wait Any Longer

DEAR NMA II

I just cannot wait any longer
Before I write you another verse
Maybe once again I am bothering you
Maybe your heart may never beat fast
Maybe this verse may never really matter
Maybe you may never want to see me again
Maybe you may never understand me
Maybe you may think am standing
In the way of your cherished ambition
10   Perhaps you are too young and innocent
To understand that I never mean any harm
Despite everything I wish to reassure you
That you may despise me if it pleases you
You may not want to see me if you so wish
You may feel am crazy if it helps you out
You may even hate me if it brightens your day
You may never think or remember me
You may choose to be indifferent after all
Though I know I want you to succeed
20   I know I want you to be happy
I know I am thrilled by the burning ambition
Pulsating in your youthful girl's heart
I know that I even take time off
To pray for you
I know that even if
You may never love me
Even if you may

Never call me "dear"
Even if my name
30 May never ring a bell
Even if my exploits
Never stir your youthful heart
Even if my poems
Never reached your shelves
Even if my tears
Never touched your heart
Even if the news of my illness
Never mattered to you
Even if you never sent me
40 A birthday card
Even if I die
Dreaming only of you

I know that I will always love you
For true love never knows any wrong
For my love for you
Is pure like the clouds
For my love for you
50 Is as innocent as a child
For it is not an infatuation
In an alcoholic intoxication
For many a time
I do remember you very fondly
For many a time
You have greatly inspired me
For you have inspired me
To sit and write all night long
Many verses, many poems
60 Epics I call my masterpiece
Many verses you may desire
To read if you so wish
Poems like "In Our Little Ship—*The Argosy*"
Poems like "The Love We Shared"
Verses like "Dear Nma I"
Written on the shores of the Atlantic

On my last trip to Lagos
Verses like "Ripples in My Bathtub"
Written in faraway Rimi, a desert countryside
Which one will I say?
Which one will I not say?
Though I do know
That the winds of time
Do always change the hearts
And the minds of men
You see it is neither your fault
Nor is it my own
For the response to love
80   Knows no bounds
You could ask the trees
And the leaves of grass
You could inquire from
The waves of the sea
You could ask the birds of the air
You could well question
The busy wings of the bee
You could ask the butterflies
On the petals of rose
90   You could well ask
The ears of the winds of time
Please do ask the siesta flies
You could even ask the mosquitoes
That sometimes disturb your princessly sleep
You could ask the innocent
School children on the roadside
Do well ask the doves
The holy birds
Do well inquire from
100   The grasshoppers in your lawn
Do well ask the silent
Walls in your room
Please do question
The ears of your pillow
You could ask

The tears from my eyes
You could ask the silent stones
The rock and the sea
You could ask the shells
110   From the seashore
Please do ask the silent
Ears of a lonely road
You could ask the ripples
Of the flowing stream
For you could ask
The lines of my verses
Do well question the beauty
Of the petals of rose
You should well ask
120   Whosoever you wish
For all will tell you the same
That I am in love
Not in love with the princess
Of Prince Charming
Not in love with the princess
Of the Sleeping Beauty
But in love with a princess
Which you are
A princess from Eluama
130   Where Elegant Daughters grow
A princess from Eluama
The heartbeat of my creativity
For my heart is busy
And quite occupied thinking of you
For you may take all the time
In the world to succeed
To pursue your ambition
To its diminishing returns
Let nothing stop you
140   For the sky is your limit
For come rain come sunshine
My love for you
Will never die

For I am not ashamed
Of falling in love
Here at home a second time
For my name is love
For my name itself is in love
For I am not in doubt
150   Of falling in love with you
Thought somebody or nobody
I may really be
Though how young
You may be at heart
It could never come in between
My endless love for you
Your love,

6:30 am
July 8, 1993
Block 84, Flat 3
OAU Summit Quarters (Comoros)
Asokoro, Abuja

I AM SORRY FOR EVER KNOWING YOU

DEAR NMA III

It is my sincere wish instead
To let you know how much
I do regret for ever knowing you
I want it to register in you that
I am sorry for ever knowing you
Many girls here in Karu do wish
Indeed very greatly to win my heart
When they visit me they buy me fruits
With their own hard earned money
10   They are very happy when I offer them a seat
They are very pleased when I talk with them
They are abundantly thrilled to read my poems
They wonder very greatly whom you must be
Who this wonder girl must be?
They say you must be a lucky girl
Whose luck rings a bell in my brain
Who does not seem to understand
The magnitude of love that I have
Who takes pride in tormenting my heart
20   Many a time they are unhappy with me
Why I should fall in love with you?
In the first stance, and why
You take solace in paying me back with scorn?
They wished very greatly to see you
And tell you how lucky a girl you must be
I do not invite them to my house

But they just come on their own
Most of the time they come to read my poems
Sometimes they wear my apron and enter my kitchen
30   Sometimes they make me some soup and stew
Sometimes they want to put food into my mouth
Sometimes they wished I could fall in love with them
But many a time I told them about you
Many a time they inquired to see your picture
Many a time I tell them I do not even have one
That you have bluntly refused to send me one
That you do not want me to see your face
That you are cross and bitter with me
For falling head over heels in love with you
40   Then they tell me to let you lose in the winds
That you are not the only girl in the world
That there are many beautiful and brilliant girls
Who are many times better than you are
That I should forget you for good
That you are a very ungrateful girl
Who may never fall in love with the right guy
They sometimes want to despise me for loving you
Because I tell them that I love you very much
I tell them that you have stolen my hart
50   And that you have hidden it in your bosom
That there is virtually nothing I can do
Except to wait and hope that one day
You could grow up to remember me
And then turn around to search for me
With the conviction and truth of someone you love
But the days are passing away very fast
And I am getting older than you know
I do very much want someone to carry my babies now
And I do need someone to be their mother
60   I need someone to look upon now
As the future mother of my anticipated babies
I need someone to love
I need someone to love me back
I want to live a clean life

So that God will not be angry with me
And decide to shut up the gates
Of my endless inspiration to write
Then I found out that I am young
That I am young and strong
70   That I am greatly in love
With a virgin girl who cares for me less
And that I could not love someone else
That no one else stimulates my love
That no one else makes any meaning to me
Because you are truly my heart
Because you are truly my love
Though you do not seem to understand
Though you do not value the power of love
Maybe because you have never fallen in love
80   Maybe because you spend most of your time
With no one else but your junior brother
Maybe because you are afraid
Of what your junior brother will say
Maybe you are afraid of your junior brother
Maybe you fear that he will tell your mum
That you are in love with a guy
Who is a few years older than you are
Maybe you do not understand that you can love
That you can love someone from purity and innocence
90   Maybe all your ideas about love is marriage and sex
Maybe you do not know that love transcends
That love transcends all boundaries
That true love has very little to do with sex
That true love is a love of innocence and purity
That my love for you is pure and innocent
And that this is the reason why it is productive
This is the reason why it has truly
Changed the value of love today
From the concept of sex and immorality
100 To the noble art of creativity
That true love yields positive fruits
While fake love makes a girl pregnant

True love never hurts the heart
True love never spoils useful habits
True love helps to build the barriers,
The rocky walls against the urge for immorality
Though I do not claim to be a moralist
But the essence of my moral lessons
Is to let you know that your fears are empty
110   Your mum could know that I love you dearly
Your father could know that I am crazy about you
Your brothers could know that you inspire me
To write all night long and all day long
Your family will be thrilled that you are a source
Of some noble inspiration which pours out at all times
To water down the feelings and emotions of men
I guess these things you do not know
And as such you have treated me very badly
As such you have been very mean to me
120   As such you have worked hard to kill the love
Yes, the youthful love that burns in me
It hurts very much I must not fail to say
To tell you once again how it feels
To love someone who never cares a bit
For I am really sorry for ever falling in love with you
For you go and mark it down somewhere
Any man who says he loves you
In any form he likes to use
Could not near my unreserved love
130   For your loveless mortal heart
I am indeed sorry for ever knowing you
Unendingly
Your love,

2:20 pm
January 14, 1994
Karu, Abuja

I AM SORRY FOR LOVING YOU

DEAR NMA IV

For the past four months
I have decided to start writing
My free-styled unsealed love letters
Which are never posted anymore
Because I want to keep them to myself
Because I want to reverse this ugly trend
And start loving myself instead of the wind
I have in each occasion gone to Area 10
Yes, to the UTC stores at Area 10, Garki
10   There I usually go each month I finished
Writing one of these my unsealed love letters
I go to UTC stores and buy myself a present
I choose one or two good things, I felt
I would have loved to buy for you
This monthly ritual now reassures me
That I am now falling in love slowly
With myself first, then any other person could follow
This time around at the UTC stores
I saw a mug on display
20   The price tag is fifty-five naira
Which is equivalent to about one dollar
In our Nigerian black market
Then I turned the mug around
It was beautiful and well made
But my heart skipped a little
Like when I was in Rimi of Katsina
When I used to receive your mails

Then I saw that on it is a rose flower
And the inscriptions "Love"
30   All what struck me was "Petals of Rose"
And all the evocation you have inspired in me
Then my heart was beating quite fast
Then I lifted the mug with my left hand
Which you know too well is my own right
And I scrutinized the mug very closely
The artist did a perfectly finished job
On the creation of the rose on the mug
Then I knew it was meant for me
Because this time around you don't exist
40   For I have convinced myself that you have gone
That you have gone on a long train journey
That your case is closed for good
And all that remains is essentially for me
To turn my love around to myself
So I bought the mug for my morning coffee
For each morning I prefer to use the mug
Essentially because I am now falling in love
With myself and am poised to make good of it
But one significant thing happened at UTC stores
At the point I lifted up this mug in admiration
50   I sighted a young late teenage girl just like you
I was even scared whether it was you
But with the corner of my eyes in pretext
I observed that it was not you
Because her hair was longer than yours
Before I could finish scrutinizing the mug
She came much closer with boldness
And engaged me in a slow conversation
She surprised me very much because she knew my name
She performed like this
60   "Hi, Monday is your shopping day each week?."
Then I looked up to behold this charming girl
"Do you remember me still?" she questioned
"Am afraid, young lady, I really don't"
I replied with my usual confident self

"Don't you remember Maggie?" and she giggled
"I was at your hospital yesterday," she continued
My mind flashed back to my duty yesterday
And I remembered having met a pretty girl like her
Then I pretended that all is well
70   And replied in affirmative
Then she continued
"That's a nice mug
Are you buying it for your heartthrob?
Or is it just to remind you about her
As you seemed so absorbed
While you examined the mug
With some precision like you did to me yesterday."
I was a bit uncomfortable in there
Because I hated being toasted by a girl
80   I excused myself and requested that we talk outside
She obliged me with radiant smiles
I felt that was a good opportunity for me to escape
I quickly took my mug to the counter
Paid for it and started off for home
Lo! And behold was Maggie at the doorstep
Then we talked and talked and talked at length
She did not want me to go again
She succeeded in finding out everything
Yes, everything about the rose and the mug
90   I had to tell her because I really needed someone
Yes, I needed someone caring like Maggie to talk to
She asked me to buy one of such mugs for her
Then I hesitated and she changed her mind
And said why doesn't she buy me something?
Yes, something for my birthday as I had
Told her that tomorrow is my birthday
Then she ran into the store and bought me
A brilliant white towel
She said I should use it whenever
100   I want to forget that someone is hurting me
That the towel is a reversal of my love lore
That as long as I keep it with me

That a feeling of a positive love will come to me
Then I looked at her very closely
She looked as pretty as my own Nma
She sounded as brilliant or more than you are
She is obviously a very ambitious girl
Aspiring to become a pediatrician
After her undergraduate medical training
110   She obviously know more than I imagined
She is as young as a lamb
Then she told me a lot about herself
She said she admired me in the consulting room
That I was looking really young and professional
That she would like us to be friends
And when I told her that I am planning
To join the Philatelic Club in Abuja
She jumped to the sky with joy
Saying that she is a member and already
120   Has gotten more than hundred different Nigerian stamps
And one hundred and fifty from other parts of the world
I marveled and really envied her
Because I stupidly gave out my eighty-nine stamps
From different parts of the world to my friend's sister
Because I was entering college and felt
Such things like stamp collection are for kids
But now I know that they are for adults as well
Then Maggie told me in a blunt language
That she is in love with me first time
130   That when she saw me in the clinic, she fell in love
She told me she is as young as a lamb
That she is as free as the air
That she is as single as a spinster
That she is equally as innocent and as pure
And that she is still equally a virgin
Because I told her that you are a virgin
And that this is one of the reasons why
You inspire me endlessly
She told me how much she wished

140   She could fit into your shoes
       That she would want me to give her my heart
       So that she could keep it for me
       And that she will give me back all the love
       I have been searching for all my life
       Then she told me that her sister was my mate
       That her senior sister was my mate in high school
       That her sister has a very sound knowledge
       Concerning my exploits at school
       And that she talks about me very highly
150   I looked at her very closely again
       She is as fair as, but fairer than you are
       Her skin is also as soft and as tender
       Her face looks innocent and pure
       But her face is not as round as yours
       She is a charming teenage girl
       Though she lacked this gripping aura you exude
       But then I made up my mind
       That I was going to give her a chance
       For the first time since I set my eyes on you
160   I was moved to love another girl
       Yes, to love another girl in reciprocation
       Yes, to love another girl in retaliation
       Yes, to love another girl who cares for me
       For true love is reciprocal—a game of give and take
       True love is not selfish like you are
       So that now Maggie is walking slowly into my heart
       Though I am allowing my head first before my heart
       And I still want to tell you that
       I am indeed sorry for ever loving you
170   A love you can count on

       9.30 pm
       September 23, 1994
       Karu, Abuja

I Didn't Create Myself

Dear NMA V

It is twelve midnight
The night is pretty cold
For the Harmattan is in the air
The whole place is so quiet
That a pin-drop on a bed of cotton wool
Will be loud enough to wake the cat
I just had a short walk
To summon enough inspiration
To write one of these verses for myself
10   Here I am sitting on my reading table
With my writing papers scattered here and there
I am wearing my slightly oversized
"Indeed" cardigan made by Hilton
It is pretty warm for the cold weather
My aim is essentially
To tell you about myself
For I am convinced
That you know very little
About my humble self
20   I am not really attempting to write
My autobiography per se
But merely to acquaint you a little
About my humble origin
For maybe that may give a clue
To the explosion of love in me
The story I am going to tell you
My senior brothers and sisters did tell me

That I was born in a remote countryside
Whose name is after that of a river
30   That the place is a local railway station
Near the largest plateau in Nigeria
The time of the day or night
That I was born, no one could remember
The exact day of the week
And month was not known
All they could remember is the year
And as such I have discovered interestingly
That even number years are my years
Because many great things in my life
40   Happen only on even number years
And for the first time in my whole life
Of twenty-eight years presently
I confirmed that the even numbers are mine
I won a lucky-dip prize purposely
By picking an even number from the tray
Of many odd and even numbers
However, when I went to school
My date of birth was registered
With an odd number year
50   The reason was not clear to me
But I guessed it must have been an oversight
From that initial registration
I observed that I was born
On November 19
And I have had to write eighteenth at times
The reason again I do not know
It was said that I had a mother
And she died when I was two
I learnt that she was a great woman
60   A very strong African woman
Who was an energetic farmer
And a very wealthy trader
Who sold smoked fish whole sale
In bags, in big, big bags!
To the smaller petite traders

Who patronized her goods?
She was said to be fair skinned
With an immaculate set of teeth
She was said to have an infectious mile
70 A very cheerful and friendly lady
I could not remember her face
Though I tried to stretch my memories
To the time I was breastfeeding
But I could not recollect a thing
I became the last surviving member
Of her numerous children—a football team
Though I could only see four others
With me making the number five
Others may have joined her
80 In various circumstances I do not know
But I survived the hard times
I survived the war, the horrors of war
Then you were not yet born
I survived the Nigeria-Biafran war
Which lasted for thirty months
Then I was living with my grandmother
We were camped in our farm
And sometimes we killed a goat
And sometimes we roasted some yams
90 And some cocoyam, which we ate
With red palm oil spiced with pepper
Yes, some green and red pepper
That is all I could remember
I also remembered that sometimes
When an airplane is coming
Everybody takes cover flat on the ground
And people never wear white shirts
For fear of being spotted by enemy planes
So you can see I survived hard
100 I survived from the age of two without a mother
The ugly truth you must know
Is that your face fits perfectly
With the description of my mother's face

Her pictures never survived the war
So I could never tell what she is like
Then the older members of my family
Took some time to describe her face
"Her face fits into my senior brother's"
But my senior brother is a man
110   None of my sisters has her face
But they have her physique
The sum of all the descriptions
I have here in my head
Fits exactly into most of your features
This is the naked truth
And an open secret
Which I have let out today to the world
And this is possibly the reason
Behind my endless love for you
120   For the memories of a mother
I never really had
Lingers hard in your virgin heart
For my love of the mother
I never had, I craved greatly from you
For the mother's care I never had
I blindly sort from you
I expected you to grow overnight
I expected you to read my mind
I must have been indeed
130   Expecting too much from you
An inexperienced late teenage girl
Who does not know her left from her right
From the wrongs and right
You are like some innocent chicks
Who have merely hatched
From the shells of her eggs
Into our harsh world
Only to find herself
Been bashed left, right, and center
140   With all kinds of words and presents
In the sweet name of love

Which you have not even tasted
You do not know how sweet
Or how bitter this love can be
And as such you are careful
So as not to be derailed prematurely
I admire your comportment
I admire your patience
But be that as it may
150   I did not create myself
And neither did you create yourself
For you and I are mere accidents
In the hands of the creator
Fitting into different times
Fitting into different backgrounds
But growing to find a common ground
A common neutral ground for interaction
And that neutral ground is my love
And my love is your being
160   And your being is the composite bundle
A bundle composed of a great package
A package interwoven with the accident of history
Compounded by the desire to be loved
Which crystallized in an attempt to create
And you proved to be the source
An inspirational source of intense value
Which has enkindled a candle flame
In my creative noble psyche
Possessing me from time to time
170   From moment to moment
From day to day
From time and time again
And you have proved greatly
To become the fountain source
Of an endless stream of thoughts
Some endless imaginations
Which have found solace
In the pages of books
And I reason that you must marvel

180　"Why me of all persons
　　　To have been the one
　　　To inspire this young man greatly
　　　And why is it that when he saw
　　　The crescent green Kubwa Hills
　　　Then his memory cells were greatly reactivated
　　　At the very time he missed me greatly."
　　　These are all the questions
　　　That could bother your little head
　　　But even my poor self
190　Does not have the answers
　　　Because I did not create myself
　　　Just like you too did not
　　　Equally have a hand in making yourself
　　　We were all made by the hand of God
　　　With a purpose perhaps we do not know
　　　But the truth remains that you try
　　　Yes, you try to understand my feelings
　　　You try to understand my problems
　　　You try to understand my history
200　You try to understand my birth
　　　And all the circumstances surrounding them
　　　For now you could see
　　　That I adore you
　　　Not because you are Venus
　　　The Roman goddess of love and beauty
　　　But because you happen to represent
　　　The softest spot in my existence
　　　You represent one very dear object
　　　One highly valued object
210　And that is the love of my mother
　　　For I could do anything
　　　To feel my mother's hands on my head
　　　For I could give every penny I have
　　　To behold her unique pretty face
　　　For I could write all day and all night
　　　With every pronouncement from her mouth
　　　If only I could hear her speak out

I could paint her face with words
I would cover myself with her wrapper
220   I will keep a lock of her hair in my box
I will hang her pictures everywhere
Yes, in every corner of my room
I will live with her all my life
I will tape her voice and keep
And play it over and over again
It would inspire me greater than the green Kubwa Hills
It would inspire me into the mountain clouds
It will spur me on into the dead of the night
It would have made a different man of me

230   For I miss my mother very dearly
For there is only one person I miss
Like I have missed my mother
That single person is you—Nma
For you are my dreams
My great dreams of lost love
My love which was once lost to the winds
And brought back to me again
By the hands of the clock
For you are my endless dreams
240   For you are an entity
A living flesh and blood
Probably brought back into the world
By the benevolent spirit of Ada Ada
My sweet and favorite mum
For by the wings of the winds
She went on a voyage
Though a very painful one
But by the benevolence of time
Yes, the winds of time
250   Through the hands of the clock
And the accident of our lives
I was dropped in your island of love
Where I could drink from the endless springs
Yes, the fountain springs of love

Flowing and flowing endlessly
Flowing down to the east of green Kubwa Hills
Yes, flowing down to the east of Eden
Where the spring of love on earth
Was caused to ripple blues at first
260   By the benevolent hand of God
For in you I have found a fulfillment
Of the love and care never tendered
The mother's hand of love never stretched
The mother's look of love never sighted
The mother's act of love never rendered
Yes, in you, in your composite self
In the flesh and blood in you
Have I found that craving fulfillment
Though my sixth sense tells me
270   That for some time you may not understand
But my early morning prayers
Continuously look heavenward
In supplication to the Almighty
To give me your heart for keeps
For all I do know inside me
You are the love I have missed
Yes, the craving love I have missed
Since I observed that the leaves of grass
Have always been green
280   And that the sky is always blue
And that the clouds are always white
And sometimes there may be little puppies
Thatlive in the white clouds
And whenever the wind blows
The puppies grow wings and fly away
To distant lands I do not know
For if there is any single thing
That my heart could want in my life
But could never get to my yearning
290   It has never touched me that you are
But if it turns out to be so
I will give my heart to the winds

So that she could keep it for me
For to live on and on
Without your love in my heart
Will amount to living an unfulfilled life
A partial life deeply marginalized
A life of nothing but chasing the winds
A life of unfulfilled dreams
300   But if there is anything I crave
To be mine in the nearest future
It is your love, your endless love
For I do not know how much
You could tell your friends about me now
Though I believe I am no more a stranger
To your virgin heart
Ever your love

1:15 am
January 15, 1994
Karu, Abuja

PLEASE FORGIVE ME

DEAR NMA VI

Many times I have written you
To tell you how much I love you
Many times I have resisted the urge
Yes, the temptation to love someone else
But I have persevered waiting for you
It has not been quite easy with me
I have battled day by day
I have persevered week by week
I have endured month after month
10   Hoping that one day you will yield
The months are fast running across
The years are not much to my reach
My poor helpless self have been depleted
I cannot anymore withstand the urge to resist
For the pressure for me to love other virgins
Is mounting too high on my lovesick heart
I do not know what to do
I am so confused and very uncomfortable
The truth though is that
20   I will love you to eternity
But it seems that the love
Will only transcend our spiritual world
Where the psyche of your virgin heart
Has married my muse on top of the green Kubwa Hills
For I believe very strongly
That I must have been born on a hill
For my kindred were not only from the hills

But they were born at the peak of the plains
For when our minds sleep
30 They do so on top of hills
For when our minds work
They come down to the valleys
For down the valleys, the waters
Flow endlessly in great floods
Watering our dry throats
Wetting our clouded brains
Opening up many channels
Through its numerous crevices
For the endless flow of inspiration
40 For of late I have been scared
That my love for you may vanish
Into the invisible hands of the winds
For I have dreamt dreams
On this day when dreams were born
In our spirit world
Where you married my muse
For I have worshipped you endlessly
At the top of the clouded green Kubwa Hills
For I have looked for you everywhere
50 For I have sent the kites
For I have sent my friend the wind
For I have also pleaded with the power eagle
To go to the distant lands to find you
But they came back with nothing
They returned without news of you
You denied them access to your chamber
You refused them entrance to your palace
You blocked your ears with cotton wool
So that you could not hear their calls
60 For then the times are running out
For then the hands of the clock
Are moving pretty fast
The hands of the clock
Are not waiting for anyone
And the tongue of the winds

Have told me that I will stagnate
If I stay at one corner waiting for you
I have not sinned to plead for forgiveness
But I foresee the possibility in the future
70   For you have given me your deaf ears
Nma, my love, what will I do?
You have neglected me for too long
You have been very unkind to me
You have been very mean to me
You have treated me like a piece of rag
Which you know too well that am not
You have abandoned me in the colds
To the mercy of the disease of the chest
You have not for once listened to my cry
80   And now I cannot cry anymore
There are no more tears in my eyes
My tear glands have gone dry
And I have not reserved any
For the use in the rainy day
You have sapped me dry
Leaving no pulp or juice
For anyone who may care
You have used me and dumped me
You have betrayed me in the open
90   You have disgraced me in the public
Because everybody now knows
That I am head over heels in love
Yes, that I am crazily in love with you
Though I am not ashamed
But the truth remains
That I cannot endure to wait any longer
Your heart has lost the luster
Of the golden royal crown
Borne by the ballpoint of my pen
100   And somebody who understands
What it means to love
Has shown deep interest and devotion
To win the ballpoint of my fountain pen

My heart is heavy and troubled
For I do not know what to do
For I do not know what to tell
The numerous inhabitants on top—green Kubwa Hills
The leaves of grass will be aggrieved
The bark of trees will weep
110   The rocks will melt away
In sheer act of depression
The Harmattan wind will blow
And dry off the greenness at the top
Of the muse-laden crescent green Kubwa Hills
For the brooks themselves will dry
And there will be no more songs
The ripples of the brooks will cease
To sing their songs to the pebbles
The innocent beds of the brooks
120   Will not any more bubble like before
The reason looms heavily in my heart
For even me, I and myself do not understand
For another virgin not born on the plains
Another virgin born and bred on green Kubwa Hills
Not a legitimate elegant daughter of Eluama
Has given her virgin heart to me
I am really scared to accept
But her innocent heart is so caring
Her virgin heart so understanding
130   Her clean heart so loving
Her love is as great and as high
As the peak of the crescent green Kubwa Hills
Nma, please help me now
Call my spirit back by accepting me
Do not let me drop off an alien
Nma, you know how much I care
You know how much I love you
Nma, you must waste no time
You must take what belongs to you
140   You must uphold your birthright
You must take our great share

You must not let go the golden gift
For the truth of the gift lives on
The unknown truth that gold
May be mined in all soils
Around the globe by human adventures
But my golden pen is only mined
And where else, except from the Nicety Mine
For the Nicety Mine is hidden
150   In a secret vault on top of green Kubwa Hills
And only your activation of my muse
Could trigger it in response
To trace the secret path to the evocation
For when you refuse my golden pen
For when you kill the muse
Which activates my golden pen
Then there will be no oscillation
To stimulate the door of the secret literary vault
And no human could reach this treasure
160   For the treasure have been hidden from men
From time and time again
For many past centuries
Men have sought the secret
To opening this treasure cellar
But it has remained an illusion
It has remained a mirage for centuries
But the muse of my fountain pen
Has promised something new
Only when you accept your golden gift
170   Will this great legend come true
For you could as well plunge
The entire human race into this search
Into endless search in dismay
For the secret door to the hidden treasures
My dear Nma, my heart is heavy
And I am pleading for you to pardon me
Please forgive me if I sinned against your virgin heart
If out of my imperfection and craze to love
And your blunt refusal to answer my pleas

180   Fall into the virgin hands of the alien princess
You must learn to please forgive me
For she was born a princess
For her father was not a king
Neither was her mother a queen
But when she was born
Her father named her princess
Though her skin is not as smooth as yours
Her hair is not as long as yours
And her heart is not as mean as yours
190   Her heart is softer than feather
Her thoughts are gentle and caring
Her posture is a humble one
But her brain is hotter than yours
She is a firebrand thunderstorm
Determination is her daily meditation
She is as strong as an eagle
She is as caring as my mother
She is as loving as the finger pulps
She is as romantic as Ms. Naomi Campbell
200   She is as good as love herself
And she is as innocent as a dove
And her innocence most times rings a bell
And sometimes falls off the apple cart
I am scared for the way I feel
I am afraid I may yield
To her pleas and innocent fingers of love
As you have bluntly refused my great proposal
Please do forgive me if I sinned against you
Your true love
210

12:00 midnight
January 17, 1994
Garki, Abuja

I WILL REALLY MISS YOU

DEAR NMA VII

My conscience, my dynamic noble conscience
Has espoused the ethos of living in me
Making me feel sad and unfulfilled
For opting to yield to external pressures
For the reason of your increasing neglect
My inner self is battling
With decisions and indecisions
Though I still crave for you very much
But my flesh and my blood is in need
10   Is greatly in dire need of love
My spirit could keep you with the wind
But my blood and flesh are jealous
They are starved unnecessarily
As I struggle to live to my vow
Every other day that passes through
My spirit is greatly aggrieved
My mind is heavy and emotionally laden
My feelings are clouded and heavy
And when you fail to play your part
20   My emotionally lovesick heart
May opt to fall like rain for a relief
At the peak of the crescent green Kubwa Hills
For I have fought a losing battle
For I have endured to withstand the rains
For I have withheld the heat
I have survived the emotional drought
And withstood the hardships of trying moments

Forging ahead with great optimism
Praying to the winds of time
30   That you would grow up to learn
That you would grow up to fall in love
That you would grow up to understand
That you would grow up to fall in love
So that you could wipe the tears
The diamond tears from my eyes
For I have waited for too long now
For it seems that you may never love me
For it seems that all my yearnings
To hold your innocent virgin hands
40   And kiss your soft and tender lips
Fall on your immortal deaf ears
And my dreams of endless love
Could never come to pass on the hills
For if you allow my tears to fall as rain
On top of the panoramic green Kubwa Hills
Then the virgin scenes could lose their charm
Then the panorama will be no more
Then the queen of the crescent green Kubwa Hills
Will cease to commune with me anymore
50   And then the endless inspirations starved
May then quench the glow of the candle flame
For the candle flame is the flame of love
The flame of love that glows in me
For whenever the glow fades away
From the peak of the green Kubwa Hills
Then my urge to love will cease
For I will be transformed out of your reach
For I may cease to exist in your mortal world
Where words are the ingredients of love
60   Where lines grow like fruits on tree tops
Where angels sing songs on tree tops
And blue smoke rises to the sky
And caress the walls of our hearts
In romance of an endless love
While the smoke and the trees

Dance an innocent dance of the forest
In great resonance to the sweet melody
From the songs of the angels on trees
For at times our minds ripple blues
70   For at times our emotions become full
For at times they spill out in anticipation
In great expectations of an enduring time to come
That what so seems far, may come near
For my fears are too worrisome
That if the glow of the enduring love
Existing inside my mortal self
Should for any reason cease to glow
Then my mortal self would transcend
Beyond the other side
80   Where there is no love
Where love which exists is not intoxicating
Where the real love is a universal commodity
Found in all nooks and crannies
And nobody spends all his time and money
Pleading for love endlessly in futility
Truly your love

11:30 am
January 18, 1994
Karu, Abuja

I Don't Know What To Do

DEAR NMA VIII

I have been meditating very keenly
I have been very worried of late
I have been really confused
I have been really undecided
About many, many things
The truth is that I do not know
How to start the long explanation
I don't know what to do
I have asked all my friends
10 For advice on what to do
And they tell me to wait for you
They tell me to wait till you grow
I really just cannot wait
I frankly cannot wait for you
I cannot wait till you are twenty-three
I cannot wait till you pass your *JAMB*
I cannot wait till you enter the medical school
I just cannot wait any longer
I very much wish I could brave it
20 I wish I could come to your dad
To explain myself, my love, my real love
How can you be too young to love?
I do not want to believe all that
Why can't you love me back?
I cannot make out any reason why
Could it be that you are scared?
That I am too possessive a guy

I do not know that to be true
But the truth remains that
30   I could compromise anything
For you to say that
You really love me too
I am convinced am up to age
I need a girl, a woman
I need a woman to call my own
I need a woman to love
I need a woman to love me back
I need someone to cook my food
I need someone to give me a baby
40   I need someone to inspire me the more
I need someone to read my poems to
I need someone to pat me on the back
I need someone to call me '*dear*'
I need someone to cook for
I need someone to call honey
I need someone to look after
I need someone to think about
I need someone to come home and meet
I am really starved indeed
50   I am greatly starved for love
I cannot make up my mind
I cannot forget you like that
I have cried many times
I have devised many plans
I have pretended that am in love
With someone else
But all has not been the same
All have not done the magic
None at all seem to fit
60   And I sit here all alone all day long
And I sit here all alone all night long
And you cannot pick up your pen and paper
And just learn to write a line
Even, if it is just a "Hi!"
You happen to be so used to

Please, Nma, please am begging you
My knees are on my floor
I am begging you to come home
Even if you cannot come home now
70   Just tell me, you love me too
It is very difficult for me here
There is no happiness for me
There is no fun for me
There is no excitement for me
My heart no longer beats fast
Nothing propelling tickles my heart
I don't know what to do
Confusion has over taken my life
There are few moments of joy here
80   There are little periods of laughter here
I don't have anyone to talk to
I don't have anyone to laugh with
I don't have anyone to share my jokes
I don't have anyone to call my own
I don't know what to do
Everybody tells me to wait
Everybody says till you grow
But you have grown
You look so big
90   Even big enough to carry a twin
So when are you going to grow?
Your height now is enough growth
Your size is okay the way it is
But your mind may need some time
Which I do not seem to have
I am working now and very hard too
I can earn enough for the two of us
We can live together while you go to school
Nma, you are not too young to love
100   Please stop killing me slowly
Stop making my life miserable
Because my affection is genuine
Because my love is real

Because my aim is clear
I want you in my house
I want to read your letters
Every now and then
I want to see your picture
Every other week
110   I want to hear from you
As often as you can write
I am so confused and overwhelmed
I don't know what to do
I really do wish I could hide
I do wish I could run away
To a distant land
Where I could not remember you anymore
Sometimes I sit and query myself
"What makes you so sure that Nma
120   Will be your ideal wife?
What if she is actually lazy?
What if she is pompous?
What if she is not respectful?
What if she takes you for a ride?
What if your love for her
Makes her turn you into a slave?
Tell me what will you do?
Are you going to run away?
Are you going to ask for a divorce?
130   Are you still going to keep loving?
Like your heart greatly craves?
Answer me young man
Before you plunge yourself in hell"
"No it cannot all be true
No, she cannot be a bad wife
No, she cannot be a lazy girl
Because lazy people are not ambitious
No, she may not be pompous
But even if she has to be
140   It must come from an inner pride
An inner pride of achievement and fulfillment

For I am convinced that she is real"
I consoled my troubled soul
Nma, I cannot wait any longer
I want you to make up your mind now
You have got to accept my pleas
If you want to set me free
I am really caged in here
By the unknown, unfelt, and inexperienced love
150   You have evoked inside of me
I am really drunk to a point of intoxication
For I do not know how and why
I cannot love somebody else except you
I want to believe that
I am in a complete mess
I am in an island prison
Surrounded by fierce fighting crocodiles
I frankly don't know what to do
I have tried to pretend
160   That all is well with me
But indeed it is of no use
I have tried to keep busy
But the thought of you
Creeps in now and again
As I keep asking myself
Whether you would have grown
In these past four weeks
But I keep wondering
When are you going to grow?
170   Is it when you are twenty-five?
Is it when you have had five boyfriends?
Is it when your heart has been broken?
When your heart has had to fall into bits?
Then you learn to pick them together
In your own selfish search for love
When someone is dying for your heart
Tell me, Nma, when will you grow?
Perhaps when I have travelled away
To a distant land in search of money

180   Perhaps when I have abandoned you,
       Perhaps when I have taken another girl
       And asked her to bear my babies
       Perhaps when I will learn not to love
       And developed a heart like wood
       Perhaps when no one
       Sings songs with your sweet name
       Then you would have grown up
       It seems to me that it is a waste of time
       Life itself is a school
190   And you could learn faster
       When you have your love on your side
       For I swear to the moon and the stars
       That I will do my best
       To pass something great to you
       In the manner of the process of growth
       For I have been growing myself
       For I have grown myself
       For I have felt what it means to grow
       For I need to teach someone I love
200   Who does not need to pay for it
       For the day I will be asked to teach you
       Then one great thing would have happened
       Yes, one great thing will happen to my life
       For I don't frankly know what to do
       For I don't know where to run to
       For I don't have no more friends to discuss you with
       They are all bored and tired of hearing your name
       I have tried to listen to the wind
       But no message comes across
210   Though the truth remains
       That only you can tell me what to do
       Your endless love

       12:35 am
       January 26, 1994
       Karu, Abuja

THE DUST IS SWALLOWING MY TOES

DEAR NMA IX

It is fifteen minutes after midnight
The Harmattan has gone with the Northeast winds
The hot weather of Abuja has returned
When the fan revolves it blows hot air
These days the wind never blows
It is now a rare blessing
To feel a cool breeze passing across
Once it is six o'clock in the morning
The harsh rays of the too-early morning sun
10   Wakes me up from bed
Most of the time I pretend
That it is still night
And try to catch a little more sleep
For these days there is not much to do
When I came back from work
By about ten-thirty this evening
My mind recalled an important story
A story of my childhood
I have not told you yet
20   It humbly started like this
"At the point I realized my left
From the difference of my right
It dawned on me that I am a leftist
I went through primary school
Writing on my slate with my left hand
In one occasion some of my classmates

Found it too strange an act
That in my first one week at school
They could not bear the strangeness
30   And they had to report me to our teacher
To probably admonish me from using my left hand
As luck may have it back then
My teacher was also a left-handed man
And he never uttered a word till date
My classmates feeling defeated
Left me to fate with my left hand
When I remember our house then
It was one big cave of a mouse hole
The roof is made of some thatch
40   And in some places some zinc
The floor is an ocean of frank dust
Back then my reading table was a basket top
It was there that I learnt my ABC
It was there I learnt that there are different letters
That some are called capital letters
While the majority of others are called lowercased letters
My sister taught me that
All human names and places start with capital letters
And every word that begins a sentence
50   Starts with big or capital letter too
Then I used to marvel with my little head
At this great teachings about book
Then a few months later my sister was married
And she left home to join her husband in Lagos
I was left alone in the mouse hole of a house
Then I started to teach myself the rest
There was no one else to ask questions
Except my teachers at school
Then it occurred to me
60   That if I make my teachers my friends
I could learn a few more extras
To make up for my sister's absence
In that form I learnt to fill the vacuum
Later my father bought me a reading table

And a reading chair
Initially my legs dangled from my chair
Then later they reached the floor
When my foot rests on the floor
70 Most times the dust swallows my toes
Yes, the dust is swallowing my toes
As I read and write on my new table
I was greatly thrilled for having them
Then I suddenly discovered that
I had been growing all that while
Most times my legs never fitted well
On my wooden chair and wooden table
And I had to ask for something bigger
Then my father brought something bigger,
80 For then if there was anything I liked doing
It was playing football and fighting
My shirt gets torn every other day
My father almost has to make
A new shirt every other week
After which he bought me khaki
Which could keep the red earth
But it never gets torn
Then I learnt that fighting
Is not good enough for me
90 I would rather play my soccer ball
Than wash the plates
I was very stubborn as a child
And my stepmother never spared me
But one thing I enjoyed most
Was reading a story book
Then there were no books anywhere
There were no newspapers
And you cannot believe it
At one time my father
100 Opened his big wooden chest
Which contained everything
You could imagine with a man
There were shirts, shorts, trousers

And even ballet shoes
Made of shining black leather
There were belts, wrist watches
There were bangles and necklaces
But most vividly I remembered
Is that there was a newspaper
110   Lying right at the bottom of the chest
I quickly brought it out
And started to read with rapt joy
Most words I could not pronounce
Most words I do not know their meaning
But I was happy calling out the ones
Yes, the few I could pronounce
It was great fun to me
And I took the newspaper and kept
I did remember one name I recalled
120   The name occurred a few times
And I think that was the reason it stuck
The name is Zik
I would pronounce Zik and I wondered
What kind of word this one is
Then I did not know it was someone's name
But the only clue I had was the Z
Is a capital letter and could be someone's name
But I never heard of someone with such a name
But later when I went up higher in primary school
130   We were taught about a man called Zik
Our history book said he was a politician
And one time the first Nigerian president
Then I never knew what all that meant
Though I always remembered to fill in the gap
Whenever they ask about the first Nigerian president
Then I loved my school box
I would arrange my books straight
My ink bottle this way
My Math's rule that way
140   And no one dares touch my school box
I treated my books like the little puppies

I never allowed dust get near them
Whenever my father buys new books
I will always wrap up the cover pages
And I will smell the fresh smell
Of a new book, it thrilled me greatly
My love for my books then were obsessive
And stories go then that no one dares
Go near my school box
150   My school box has a padlock
And the key is always with me
Once, they stole my book at school
And I cried my eyeballs out
The reason for my obsession I could never tell
Then there were football matches to play
I would play football from morning till night
I only remember home when I become hungry
Or when I get a bad leg
From rough tackle by bigger boys
160   Sometimes I only come home
When I fight and get beaten up
Most times by the bigger boys
Who feel am too heady to be spared
Then it was a lot of fun
Going to fetch water from the streams
On the way we played hide and seek
Some other times we go hunting for wild fruits
Most other times we learn to swim
That was in Lake Adaoma
170   I still remembered fondly when my father
Took me there and taught me to swim
He taught me, the forward and backward strokes
He taught me how to float on water
How to swim when the current is higher
How to rescue a drowning fellow
It was one rare good moment
I hardly ever forget about my childhood
From then on we undertook adventures
To bigger streams, swimming and swimming

180   By the time we were on our way home
Our eyes will be blood red
And everybody will be scared
That we may be spanked
For staying too long away
We will all tie knots on grass leaves
And say that we have closed
The mouths of all those that will scold
But each time we got home
We were still scolded
190   And sometimes we got good strokes of the cane
Then my father used to be a little devil
When he flogs you
And you don't run
Then you are digging your grave
Now when I flash my mind back
I just marvel and sometimes laugh it off
As the events of childhood
Though I do remember them fondly
They were great moments I cherished
200   As much as your love that intoxicates me
This is my story of childhood
Telling you essentially that
"The dust is swallowing my toes as I write."
I do miss you greatly here
I hope you have not forgotten all that
My endless love

1:30 am
January 28, 1994
Karu, Abuja

SWEET TEARS OF JOY

DEAR NMA X

The time is eight-thirty in the morning
It is a Sunday morning
I had just dropped my briefcase
Slumped into my chair
Very weak and tired
I would have wanted something to eat
But I am too tired to get up and—
Enter my kitchen to cook something as—
I have just come back from work
Because I was on call last night
The night was not busy
But I couldn't get enough sleep
I was awake all night thinking
Yes, thinking about the unknown
My mind was carried away
To a lonely land of the unknown
I missed you so much
I have never missed you like this
In my whole life before
I found myself so lonely
I found myself so empty
So incomplete, so unfulfilled
So single, so innocent, so poor
So helpless and so much in love
I looked to the east and west
There was nowhere for me to hide
I searched from the north to the south

10

20

But my problem seems more complex
Yes, more complex than I can cope with
30 I do not want to be left empty
I am tired of living alone
I need someone in my life
I need someone to love
I need someone to call my own
But no one seems to come my way
For I have pleaded with you
To come home with me
But you have given me deaf ears
You have hardened your heart
40 You have opted to be indifferent
I do not know what to do
Worse still I am unduly bugged
By the volcanic brand of ambition in my heart
I want to go back to school
To give my ego the final boost
At the same time, I want to get married
If not married, I need an engagement
I need to be engaged to someone who cares
I want someone to accept my engagement ring
50 I want someone to look upon
Someone to think about
Someone to remember
Someone to write long letters to
Someone to share my dreams with me
Someone to talk about my feelings
Someone to share my meals with me
Someone to live my life with me
Someone to call my own
I have been searching all this while
60 But I have not seen anyone
That fits into your shoes
And I seemed to be unduly overwhelmed
By the explosive power of love
Threatening to tear me apart
I do not know what to do

I sincerely hate what is happening to me
I am so confused
I do not understand
Why it should happen to me
70 Why you cannot love me back
Even if it means to do it out of pity
Even if you do it to save my life
You could be rest assured
That God will reward you
God will reward you a thousand times
He will bless you with beautiful children
He will give you an understanding husband
A husband that will understand your moods
And give respect to them
80 Whenever there is need
A husband who will love
A husband who will respect your womanhood
A husband who will be the father
The envied father of your children
Your children who will be endowed
From your womb with the fear of God
Your children who will fear and respect you
Your children who will be crowned with knowledge
Your children who will be blessed with wisdom
90 For God will bless your home
And make it as peaceful
As the scenic innocent clouds
A home where you will live
And give praises to God
A home you will care for
A home you will respect
A home other homes will envy
A home where everybody will work
For a purposeful advancement
100 A home you will learn to call the Lilies
A home for you and me
A home for us to lay the foundation
And add the bricks one after another

With great joy and laughter too
A home where we will plant lilies
And water them to grow from grass to grace
A home to call our own
I am praying for you
That God protects you
110   From the hands of wicked men
From the hands of the Jones
From the hands of the devil
That God will cover you up
With the inspiring leaves of grass
That God will bless your efforts
Like he did to that of Ruth
That God will give you wisdom
To understand the world better
That God will shower you with kindness
120   And make milk and unique honey
Flow from your virgin breasts
That the winds of time
Will pass across your life
And leave great memories for good
That you will live a life of fulfillment
That you will live a life of joy
That your days will be filled with happiness
And sadness will not come your way
That your womb will be as fruitful
130   And grow from humility to greatness
Like the pin-drop mustard seed
That all the days of your life
Will be crowned with happiness and joy
That our hearts will be filled with love
That our actions will be laced with grace
So that when people remember your name
The streams themselves will ripple in chorus
To the thoughts and feelings of men
To the thoughts and admirations of your fellow women
140   To the blessings even from innocent little children
Who will sing innocent songs with your name

Such that even the passing bands of the wind
Will re-echo their songs of praise
Now I have ceased to be pessimistic
Now I believe only in you
For my sixth sense tells me to endure
That a time will come
A time not too long
An enduring time
150   When you would have added
More weeks, more months
Filled with experiences and understanding
This will endure to mature with the years to come
The years ahead of us
The years to come in future
The one day you will remember me
The one day you will ask about me
The one day you will look for me
The one day you will read the petals of rose
160   And then you will witness
The difficult times I passed through
You will feel the power of love
That has possessed me all this while
You will know that I mean well
You will know that I have good intentions
You will then ask "Where is he?"
You will run to the top of Kubwa Hills
In search for me
You will look for the wind
170   You will go to the nest of the kites
You will visit the power eagle
And you will commune with the clouds
Asking them about me
Pleading with them to find me
For then you will close your eyes in sleep
And you will find yourself
In a new world
Dripping with the songs of love
A new clean and virgin world

180 Where you will be welcomed to the green Kubwa Hills
  By the clapping of hands
  From the innocent virgin girls
  When the queen of the crescent green Kubwa Hills
  Will conduct a choir
  And the soprano from the ripples
  Yes, from the ripples of the brooks
  Will hold an audience in rapt attention
  A choir where the wind will sing
  A choir where the leaves of grass will echo
190 The voice ringing out from the audience
  A choir where violin will play
  And the players will display
  The most intricate skills therein
  For the time will come
  When innocent little virgin girls
  Will carry flowers in white baskets
  And follow you behind
  When you descend from the green Kubwa Hills
  For then the rocks will ring their bells
200 The bells will ring on that day from the hills
  And sweet tears of joy will flow
  Yes, tears of happiness and joy
  Will drop from your virgin eyes
  And your immaculate gown
  Will thrill the envying single girls
  And then all your friends and relations
  Will come in their hundreds
  To witness this great occasion
  And when you open your eyes
210 You will be in safe hands
  In my own hands right inside our home
  Where the lilies of love will grow
  Where the lilies of love from you and me
  Will grow endlessly to produce younger lilies
  Whom we will tender with care
  Whom we will water with care
  Whom we will love for ever

For then the great and enduring dreams
The never-ending dreams
220   Flowing in the petals of rose
Will come to pass
And even the angels themselves
Yes the angels in the heavens
Will sing and make merry
While they listen to the melodies
Of the choir of virgin girls
Who will sing at the peak
Yes, at the peak of the green Kubwa Hills
Where you will marry my muse
230   Where you will transform my dreams
The long dreams from my fountain pen
Into a reality for humans to behold
And then the wind will carry
Very many leaves of grass to the hills
To witness this great moment of joy
When the happiness and joy in your heart
Will spill out the world
In a sacred solemnization
Before outstanding witnesses
240   From the east, from the west
From the north and south of the globe
And I will hear the gods chattering away
Drinking in merriment to make it a reality
Dear Nma, may God bless your soul
May God bless your endeavors
And crown you a queen of the Lilies
I will continue missing you
Till the time comes
My endless ripples of love will endure
250

4:30 pm
January 31, 1994
Karu, Abuja

A Night Before The Valentine

DEAR NMA XI

Today is Valentine's Day
Today is the lovers' day
For if there is anything in this world
I wished very much to see
It's your pretty innocent girl's face
For where I could not see your face
I could be greatly thrilled by your valentine card
For I have long been expecting your valentine card
For I have waited and waited all day long
10   But none came my way since yesterday
I had gone to the post office severally hoping
I would get your mail
Hoping that St. Valentine's spirit could stir
Your feelings to show me pity for the past love
Yes, the past endless love which I have poured on you
For all the past love you have not returned
For I prayed and hoped that maybe St. Valentine
Could touch your spirit and reveal what love is
To your innocent naïve love-proof heart
20   For the sake of my lovesick heart
I had searched and searched for you
This time around not in the lonesome green Kubwa Hills
Not among the leaves of grass
Not among the huge boulders of Abuja rocks,
But this time around amongst the endless fountains
Yes, the endless fountains made by the hand of man
Splashing endlessly in the reflection of the orange light
Yes, the orange light reflecting the romantic rainbow

Yes, the romantic endless rainbow spree
30   Which could only be discerned by my lovesick eyes
For there at the Nicon Noga Hilton Hotel Abuja
I was sitting quietly at one great end in the lobby
Hoping endlessly that you could appear
Maybe with your dad who may
Have come for a conference at Hilton
I looked for you in the endless brooms of the fountains
Rotating endlessly in a romantic fashion
Reminding me greatly about the one I love
Reminding me about you, Nma, my love
40   Consoling me that I need not despair anymore
Soothing my lonely nerves in love lanes
Admonishing my youthful firebrand love
To exercise some restraint, that one day
That one fateful day you will remember me
That one fateful day you will be mine
That one day I will tread on the golden street of love
With no one but Nma in my arms without restraints
That you will come home with me to the Lilies
That you will be crowned the mistress of the Lilies
50   And the eve of the valentine passed slowly by
With my little self, coiled on my bed thinking of you
Then I slept peacefully after a hectic day's job
For I was on call a night before the valentine
So I slept late by 1:30 am
When I lay my head down to sleep
I greatly wished that no emergency comes
So that I could be allowed to sleep
Because the whole day was busy and wearisome
To my innocent and lonesome lovesick heart
60   Then I slept like I never did in my life before
And lo! And behold for the very first time
Yes, for the first time I dreamt of you in real life
For all I saw in my five hours sleep was Nma
For I saw myself a teenage boy in Eluama
Walking down the woods to an unknown destination
And appearing suddenly under the canopy of jungle leaves
I looked up and saw you and less than one pole away

And my heart jumped into my mouth pounding away
In anticipation of a rude and an unfriendly expectation
70 From your ever-neglectful and never-caring mind
I saw myself a teenage boy in my dreams
And your appearance is that of a fifteen-year-old
You looked so young, so pretty, so cute, and so happy
And you approached me with a friendly smile on your face
Contrary to my expectations you even greeted me
While I answered very eagerly and quite surprised too
Then we walked together down the wooded path
The whole world was just for you and me
There was no one else except the two of us
80 It was only the two of us walking together
Then I told you great stories I could not recollect
And you looked quite happy and really caring
Then you even held my hand as we walked
Then we talked and walked and laughed
Holding each other's hands with our clean hearts
It was the most wonderful thing that happened to me
Yes, the most exciting experience I ever had in my life
Then we kept walking and talking endlessly
I cannot recollect a single thing we talked about
90 But two of us were really thrilled and happy too
Then the tropical afternoon sun was shining on our faces
Though most of the time we were shaded by the jungle leaves
But from moment to moment as we walked down
We embraced the brightness of the tropical sun
Then I do remember that we stopped in two occasions
To listen to the soothing songs of cooing innocent birds
While you held my right hand looking so beautiful
Yes, you looked so young and so beautiful
For you are the most beautiful girl
100 I have ever seen in my whole life
I was living in my dream world, yes, in love twinkles
My mind was as peaceful as the serene white clouds
My heart was as relaxed as the quiet happy oceans
I could not believe what was happening to me
I never knew it was in a dream, in a dream world

Where I had boarded the time machine ten years
Behind time, and where I became a teenage boy
Just in a twinkle of an eye because of love
Where I endured to transform my real self
110   Into the innocence and youth of a high school boy
Where I lost my coarse beard to a smooth chin
Where I became a different man because of love
Where I may have conjured the spirit of Venus
And she transformed me into an innocent teenage boy
And then presented me to you for acceptance
Which you did with open arms and broad smiles
My heart was greatly thrilled for this rare moment
For this unique opportunity when we explored our minds,
When we walked down the path holding hands
120   When our feet thrilled the crispy dry fallen leaves
Littered all along the wooded love path we found ourselves
When we listened together to the songs of innocent birds
When we had this rare privilege to look at each other
Straight into the eyes,
When we witnessed how much love we shared
When we embraced the gentle breeze which caressed our hearts
And blow our minds in endless affirmation to our thoughts
When we were together like we never were before
When we said sweet and lovely things to each other
130   When we pleaded to the sun not to set
So that we could go on and on seeing each other
When many good things happened to just the two of us
For then I thought it was in our real world of true love
Our real world where you have denied me your love
Our world of flesh and blood, our world of age
Our world of my endless love which have never been returned
Though I keep hoping like the white clouds that one day
Yes, one day my dreams will really come true as rain
My endless love

140

8:30 am
February 14, 1994
Garki, Abjua

THE VALENTINE'S DAY

DEAR NMA XII

It is evening now
The time is nine-thirty in the night
The moon is glowing with orange beams
The night is quiet with soothing winds
I have worked all day to a breaking point
It has been a very busy day for me
And now I have come back to rest
It has been difficult for me indeed
For on getting home and refreshing
10   I walked into my sitting room and sat
Then it dawned on me very greatly indeed
That my house is empty and very lonely too
As it has always been since all these months
I remembered you and I missed you greatly
Then the thought of you lured me out
Into the street for a lonely walk
It was then I witnessed the glory of the moon
It was then that I took solace in isolation
It was then I made the moon my companion
20   It was then I pretended to fall in love
Not with any girl you may imagine
But with the affectionate orange glowing moon
Then all I wanted in the whole wide world
Is someone very dear to my heart!
Someone I want to call my own
Someone I could tell all my little secrets
Someone I could learn to call my mother

Someone to treat me like her own
Someone to love me like I never was
30   Someone to be the envied mother of my children
It is not silver or gold or fame or riches
It is just to behold the face of my Nma
The only girl that has won my heart
The only girl that my heart craves for
The only girl in my dreams
The only girl who gives me sleepless nights
For I am endlessly longing for you
For I wanted you in my arms
For I wanted to kiss your tender lips
40   For I wished to behold your virgin hands
As we walk and talk down the street
I wished to behold your innocent virgin face
So that we could talk to each other
So that we could explore our minds
And learn our differences and similarities
So that we could understand each other
Much more than words could carry
On the endless lines and pages of books
So that we could read our thoughts
50   Like Romeo and his heart-throb Juliet
So that we could share my great inspirations
Which fall cats and dogs in an overwhelming flood
Saying things like this:
"For I will build a stone house for you
Which we shall name the Lilies
I will make a home for you
Where the green leaves of grass
Sing their endless songs to the clouds
A house whose gate is called LOVE
60   A home you will be proud to invite our friends
A home where laughter and happiness reigns
A home you can call your own
A home we could share a vintage wine
A home where you are the queen and I am the king
A home where our children will be born

A home for them to call their own
A home for just the two of us
A home for you and for me
A home where we could thrash out our differences
70   And lend each other a helping hand to make amends
For the greatness of tomorrow to come"
For this afternoon when I was on break
I took a taxi to Area 1 of Garki here in Abuja
The time was three o'clock in the afternoon
I dropped at Area 1 Shopping Center
Then I visited the Home of Cards
In the Home of Cards I saw very many
Then I remembered you very greatly too
Then I missed you more than I ever had
80   Then I really missed you like I have never done before
I wished greatly I could touch your hands
I wished I could just see your face
Though that may be asking for too much
I tried to console my troubled mind
And I told myself that even if not seeing you
Nor touching the pulp of your virgin fingers
Though it could have been the greatest thrill of '94
For my eyes to behold a valentine card
Sent and signed by my love—Nma
90   But I waited all day and none came my way
Then I remembered that some time last year
When I was a poor Youth Corper
I had spent my last kobo
At UTC Stores in Kano City
To buy and send you a valentine card
A very unique and different kind of valentine card
The type of card that opens its door
With heart-melting love songs
The type of card whose words
100   Could transform anyone into a new world
Where nothing but love mattered
Then I did send it by express mail
So that it could get to you on Valentine's Day

But sad enough you could not acknowledge it
However, as things stand now
My fortunes are fast changing
For now I have enough money
Yes, I got enough cash in my briefcase
To buy you a tasty card worthy of a virgin princess
110 Which I have crowned you in the *'whispers of love'*
But I could not buy any to send to you
Because my friends blame me very greatly
For all my numerous cards that have come your way
For all the long love letters I have posted to you
They blame me for making your head swell with pride
Yes, for making your head swell like a coconut
For giving you all the opportunities
To make you feel on top of the world
For telling the whole truth in my mouth
120 For loving you like I have never loved before
For revealing the true love that flows in me
For letting the cat out of the bag too early
For loving you with all my heart
For craving for your naïve and
Inexperienced virgin heart
But upon all these endless blames
One thing I still wished greatly to do
Is to summon enough courage against my ego
To send you another valentine card
130 Then I searched and searched for a card
Yes, I searched for an ideal card for my princess
Then I saw one which says
"I missed you so much
Because I love you so much"
Then I said I will send it
Then I also saw another which I could not resist
The words on it haunted me greatly
It says "God bless you, Mother
On your birthday"
140 On this birthday card is a mother swan
With her five little ones

They are swimming across a lake
A beautiful lake full of pink-colored flowers
Floating on the green leaves of the water lilies
Near the banks of the lake is a mesh at the edge
Even on the banks of the lake
Are apple trees with inviting ripe apples
The lake flows gently southward
Toward an old Roman church
150   From a distance southward I observed
That the church has some usual features
It has four arched windows facing northwards
An entrance porch on the west side
A tower with a steeple holding a cross
And most probably harboring the church bell
At the east side is a Vestry
The painting is really close to real life
For there the sky is calm and blue
And the white clouds are nursing
160   As always, their little white puppies
Here as I stood admiring the painting
My emotions built to an overwhelming crescendo
And tears were dropping down my eyes
Before I could catch those, three
Yes, three tears of love have reached the floor
Though I was able to cover up
Before anyone could notice the drama
For here I am missing a virgin girl
Yes, a virgin girl I love so much
170   A virgin girl who has refused to return my love
For here I am missing my dear sweet mother too
Whom I do not even know
Whose picture I never saw with my eyes
For she died when I was a baby
For I have never missed her this much
For some reasons I do not know why
Then I bought this emotion-packed birthday card
And I took it home with me
At home I consoled my empty self

180	That I will address it and send it
	And I will write a long letter to my mum
	And post it into the wind
	However, when I got home
	I did address your card as well
	But neither of the two cards
	That I bought could be mailed
	I kept both to myself
	For you have wronged me greatly of late
	And for my mother's birthday card
190	I kept it standing on the table
	For it makes me feel she is here
	And consoles me each moment
	I start missing you Nma!
	Be rest assured for one thing
	For come rain or sunshine
	For come daylight or darkness
	For come good or evil though
	For come life or death
	For come poverty or riches
200	For come what may
	My endless love for you
	Could never die
	Even long after I have lived and died
	My love will always remain for you
	For wherever you may live
	In the spirit or our ephemeral world
	There my love lives on and on
	Enduring till the end of the times
210	Your friend and your love,

11:30 pm
February 14, 1994
Karu, Abuja

My Love Has Been Sealed

DEAR NMA XIII

The deed is done to the celebration of love
The die is cast to all that is written for the sake of love
The rocks are happy atop the great inspiring rolling Hills
My mind is awake to the intricacies and the labors of love
The tunes have played and endlessly too to the songs of love
The song has been hummed and tweeted by the birds of love
My love has been sealed in the eternity in the heart of man
At the top of the green Kubwa Hills
For my tears of joy are dropping down
To my endless songs of love
There is no more to say
Though my fountain pen remains wet
Dripping endlessly more and more
To fulfill my promise
That every alphabet in your name
Will evoke enduring stories
Contained in great love books
To thrill the minds of men
To thrill the minds of women
To thrill the minds of babies to grow into boys
The minds of babies to grow into girls
So the energies have been deviated
To the valleys and to the lowlands
For the hills have exhausted their muse
For I will wait as long as you grow
For I know you will come back to me
For you belong to my real world

For our stars are in love with each other
For you belong nowhere else
Except in the mutual galaxy
Of our own great stars
Which will rise and shine
When all my endless dreams will come true
For now I will take solace
In the company of my petals of rose
Growing endlessly in my country home
Located somewhere in the little town
On many inspiring soft green hills—Eluama
For this is a promise fulfilled
Fare thee well truly
Good-bye
My love

9:00 am,
February 28, 1995,
Karu, Abuja

Smithson Buchi Ahiabuike is a practicing physician in North America. He is a prolific poet, writer and critic. His literary works have been published in Nigeria, USA, and internationally. He started writing at an early age. He was born in Moroa-river of Nasarawa. He hails from Eluama Isuikwuato of Abia State Nigeria. He went to medical school at College of Medicine, University of Nigeria Enugu Campus. He is married, with four children. He lives with his family in northeast Alabama.